VERGIL'S LATIUM

Shepherd boy with sheep dog on the Roman Campagna

VERGIL'S LATIUM

By BERTHA TILLY

Ph.D., M.A. (Lond.)

Totius autem Italiae curiosissimum fuisse
Vergilium multifariam apparet
SERVIUS, *Ad Aen.*, I, 44

BASIL BLACKWELL
OXFORD
MCMXLVII

FIRST PUBLISHED 1947

M.S.C./24

PRINTED IN GREAT BRITAIN IN THE CITY OF OXFORD
AT THE ALDEN PRESS

PREFACE

THE researches of which this volume is a record were carried
out between the years 1933 and 1939. They represent topographical studies of the coastal district of the Roman Campagna (known as Latium to the Romans) with reference to the
last six books of the *Aeneid*. The majority of the photographs
were taken before 1939, but none is later than April of that
year. During the past war, the allied armies, advancing on
Rome from the south, passed through all this land, leaving
behind them the havoc and destruction of modern mechanized
warfare. It has not yet been possible to learn details of losses
or of survivals in this peculiarly Vergilian country. This mono-
graph therefore presents the Campagna in all its tranquillity,
seclusion, and beauty of pre-war days.

The opportunity of collecting the material for this book,
and of visiting the places on the Roman Campagna connected
with the last six books of the *Aeneid* was made possible by the
award, in 1933, from Bedford College for Women, of the Not-
cutt Travelling Studentship. During my stay in Italy, and on
several subsequent visits, I enjoyed residence at the British
School at Rome, a privilege for which I am glad to record my
gratitude. This book represents, in a revised form together
with some additions, a thesis approved for the degree of Doctor
of Philosophy in the University of London in 1940; its
publication has been aided by a grant from the Publication
Fund of the University of London. All quotations from the
Aeneid are taken from the Oxford Classical Text, permission
for the use of which has been very kindly given by the pub-
lishers.

To Professor H. E. Butler I owe my first expression of
thanks: he gave me unstinting help from the beginning, not
only in suggesting topography as an approach to Vergilian
studies, but in reading and criticizing my work both when in
process, and later, when in thesis form. Professor B. Ashmole
also gave his criticism of my thesis, and Mr. C. G. Hardie,
when Director of the British School at Rome, and Miss M. E.
Hirst scrutinized certain chapters. Dr. Axel Boëthius was so
kind as to explain to me in 1934 the excavations of the basilica

at Ardea. I am indebted also to Mr. C. A. Ralegh Radford, until recently Director of the British School at Rome, for detailed criticism of these papers, for many helpful discussions on controversial and archaeological points, and for going over some of the ground with me. More recently, Mr. W. F. J. Knight has been most kind in suggesting various additions and improvements; I acknowledge most grateful thanks for all the time and labour he spent on my behalf.

Lastly these acknowledgments would not be complete without some reference to those students of the British School who have been most pleasant companions on my many excursions on to the Roman Campagna.

BERTHA TILLY

Ely 1946

CONTENTS

ILLUSTRATIONS

MAPS AND PLANS

x

INTRODUCTION

THE Roman Campagna, which stretches from north of the Tiber as far south as Terracina, and eastward to the Sabine and Alban hills, with its sunlit plains, fertile valleys, and ever-changing aspects, is a land of enchantment and delight which the modern world has for the time passed by, although it lies around the very gates of Rome. There are preserved there the memorials of many ages gone, from pre-Roman to late mediae-val times, and every prospect is imbued with the spirit of an ancient and simple life. The traveller may pass over the wide and rolling grassland with only the shepherds and their flocks for companionship, and with the horned cattle and herds of horses bred on the good pastures. Always the mountains are in sight, closing in the broad Campagna, and dominated by the Alban Mount, now called Monte Cavo, and always the sea shining blue to the westward. Under a cloudy sky, the aspect can be drear and forlorn, when rain gathers from the Mediter-ranean and brings a shudder of hopelessness over the fields, but when the sun is clear, the translucence is that of another world, and the life seems truly Arcadian. This is the scene of the dramatic action of the last six books of the *Aeneid*; it is the field of strife whereon is played to its finish the struggle for the foundation of the Roman race, and for the birth of Rome. On this soil still remain the Vergilian cities of Ostia, Ardea, Lavinium, and Laurentum, and here are still to be found the sulphur springs where was Faunus' oracle, and the sacred river Numicus where the deified Aeneas was worshipped. There one can wander on the Laurentian shore amid the dunes and reaches of pale golden sand, and commune in spirit with mythical times of epic legend and romance.

From the summit of the Mount can be seen in the distance the whole setting of the *Aeneid* in Latium, as when Juno ascended to see the plain and the warring ranks.[1]

At Juno e summo, qui nunc Albanus habetur,
(tum neque nomen erat nec honos aut gloria monti),
prospiciens tumulo campum aspectabat et ambas
Laurentum Troumque acies urbemque Latini.

[1] *Aen.*, XII, 134-7.

From its height can be seen the mountain ranges which run down to the sea, and the Campagna fields chequered with rich blues and greens seeming themselves like a visionary sea, and beyond, the Mediterranean, blue as a jewel. There can even be descried, in clear light, the mound which marks the western defences of Ardea, and the tower of the Palazzo Borghese at Pratica di Mare, ancient Lavinium, the city which was not yet when Juno looked down with more than mortal sight upon the closing scene of the combat between Aeneas and Turnus.

In spring the undulating pastures, the screens of woodland, and the sunken glades and valleys are bathed immeasurably in the bountiful light of the Italian sunshine, are resonant with lark song and spangled with many a wild flower and fragrant plant. Asphodel (pl. 1) grows there luxuriantly with its long slender leaves, and stately inflorescence of misty pink and star-like blossoms, and an anchusa of a deep and brilliant blue grows in masses on the fields. The very air becomes sweeter when aromatic plants growing in the grass are trodden underfoot.

By the coast still flourishes in places the primeval maritime forest, which once covered all the shore far to the north and south. It is composed for the most part of cork-oaks, ilexes, and umbrella pines; these with their slender trunks and branching tops are twisted and spread into many a fantastic shape. In the undergrowth are scented shrubs: the rosemary covered in spring with deep lavender blossom, the *daphne* bearing rosettes of pink flowers encircled with dark green leaves, which give out a sweet and heavy fragrance, and a tall winter heath. The arbutus tree, too, grows abundantly, and the wild fig is indigenous. Many varieties of small flowers grow wild in the rich sandy soil, such as the pink cyclamen, butcher's broom, and many species of vetch, and cistus, anemone, campion, and geranium. Near the modern Via di Decima, where is now the royal chase, deer and wild boar can sometimes be seen feeding in the glades, a truly Vergilian scene, recalling the slaying of Silvia's stag in the seventh *Aeneid*.[1]

For all its beauty, there lies hidden in the bosom of this historic land a plague which has ravaged it time and again through the ages, causing it to become almost deserted at certain epochs, reducing the population, and, as a result, inter-

[1] *Aen.*, VII, 483-510.

fering with proper cultivation and care of the soil.[1] The scourge
of malaria first reached the Campagna, it is thought, in Roman
times, perhaps in the second century B.C. when the Carthaginians may have brought it from North Africa where the
anopheles mosquito, which is the bearer of this disease, is
indigenous. The stagnant waters and stretches of marshy land
found in many places on the Campagna would doubtless prove
to be suitable breeding-grounds. Malaria cannot have become
prevalent until later because under the Republic the population
of the Campagna was greater than now, and also many Romans
had villas for summer residence, even along the coast where
afterwards it was rife. Those who have studied this problem
are of the opinion that malaria varies in intensity, which would
account for the fact that history shows the Campagna to have
been more thickly populated in some ages than in others. The
Romans tried to grapple with this plague by means of drainage
and good roads, and in modern times, since as long ago as
1901, the government, assisted by the Red Cross Society, has
taken measures to hold it in check. Though not eliminated, the
prevalence of malaria had been, at least until the advent of the
war, greatly reduced, although some districts still remained
unhealthy and dangerous.

The life of the shepherds can have changed little since the
early ages, when the Campagna was first inhabited, for the
round or rectangular straw huts (pls. 2 and 4) which serve as
their homes during the winter months when the flocks are
brought down from the Apennines to pasture in the warmer
climate, recall a primitive age. Coming upon a solitary home-
stead with dwelling-place, barns, and milking-sheds (pl. 3) for
the ewes, all of wattle and straw, or a group of straw huts
clustered into a village, the traveller may well think that he is
looking at a settlement of prehistoric times newly sprung into
life. Wooden bunks ranged in three tiers round the interior are
their beds; a cauldron suspended over an open fire in the
middle of the hut serves for the cooking of their simple food,
for the most part green vegetables and *ricotta* (cheese made from
sheep's milk) washed down with thin wine. Their water-supply
is carried in oval wooden casks on the backs of mules or donkeys
from the nearest spring. The characteristic costume consists of

[1] Tomassetti, *La Campagna Romana*, 1910, pp. 68, 166; also Villari, *On the Roads
from Rome*, 1932, p. 137 sq.

sheepskin trousers, a long staff, a black slouch hat and a volu-
minous cloak for the colder weather. Their great, white, black-
eyed dogs with shaggy coats are faithful and sagacious, and
sometimes dangerously fierce to strangers. They are said to
have a strain of wolf in them, and are called *canelupi*, 'wolf-
dogs'. These shepherds[1] are of a race apart, coming mostly
from the Abruzzi, in the region of Aquila. They are of a most
kindly and friendly disposition, endued with the natural
courtesy and ease of the countryside, their characters reflecting,
perhaps, the clear sunshine and quiet of the plains over which
they roam in the care of their peaceful flocks. They will talk
with strangers with the greatest pleasure, sometimes revealing
a store of knowledge which surprises. The writer once con-
versed with one who knew the history of Ardea, which lay
about two miles away from his hut settlement.

The scenery of the Campagna and its pastoral life can be little
changed from what was to be seen and experienced in Vergil's
own days, for we have the testimony of an author writing
in the time of Trajan, less, that is, than a hundred years after
the *Aeneid* was finished. In the famous letter describing his
Laurentian villa, the younger Pliny[2] tells of the woods, the
wide pastures, and the flocks which were brought there for
winter grazing: 'varia hinc atque inde facies: nam modo
occurrentibus silvis via coartatur, modo latissimis pratis
diffunditur et patescit; multi greges ovium, multa ibi equorum,
boum armenta, quae montibus hieme depulsa herbis et tepore
verno nitescunt'.

This passage might well have been written to-day, so aptly
does it describe the features of the Campagna country as we
know it now.

There is a gulf of several hundred years, which cannot
be spanned, between the suppositional date of the Trojans'
arrival in Italy, and that of the earliest archaeological finds.
Indeed, so far, nothing so early has been revealed anywhere in
the coastal belt which extends from Ostia to the south of Ardea.
Although human habitation did not reach the plain until the
first phases of the Iron Age, remains of former ages have come

[1] For an interesting account of modern conditions on the Campagna, see Villari,
On the Roads from Rome, 1932, especially chap. VI.

[2] Pliny, *Ep.*, II, 17, 3. He was in his eighteenth year at the time of the great eruption
of Vesuvius which destroyed Pompeii in A.D. 79 (*Ep.*, VI, 20, 5), and is considered to
have died in A.D. 111.

PLATE 1. Asphodel growing on the Roman Campagna (see page xii)

PLATE 2. A typical *capanna*, or straw hut (see page xiii)

PLATE 3. Milking-sheds for the ewes (see page xiii)

PLATE 4. A *capanna* being constructed (see page xiii)

to light on the Alban hills. Neolithic man[1] settled only sparsely here and there on their western ridges, as finds from graves clearly show, and it may be that lingering volcanic activity in these hills, where in fact the lakes of Nemi and Albano are seen to be extinct volcanic craters, retarded his cultural development. After a long interval came settlers of the late Bronze Age,[2] who, however, like those before them, did not descend to the plain. The flat coastland was, in prehistoric times, in all probability thickly wooded and swampy, and it is possible that human settlement only became possible when the Iron Age men, with their stronger tools and possibly more robust physique, could make clearings in the thick tree-growth and some attempt to drain the marshy land. We must conclude that the Campagna plains were not inhabited by man until the eighth century B.C., and that until then its appearance was that of a tract of primeval forest and marsh with rocky plateaux standing clear here and there where the Villanovans made their first primitive settlements, but settlements which were late in Italian prehistory. Thus archaeology does not confirm the tradition that either Ardea or Lavinium was an inhabited site in Trojan times, or that they could, in reality, have played any part in the Aeneas-legend.

An epic poet writing of a well-loved country, and of well-loved scenes, cannot have failed to reproduce that which must have been imprinted in the visual thought by inspiration and attraction. That land lying outside the gates of the Mother City must have been known to all who had an eye and a heart for the other-worldliness of its life and atmosphere. Even as it was seen and loved by Pliny, so the greatest of all lovers of the pastoral must have known and loved it. Over the ancient places which Vergil knew and which inspired him, the poet threw a shining veil of phantasy, making the ruined villages the storied homes of heroes and of champions, the rustic cults sanctuaries of great and tutelary gods, and the shepherds' peaceful fields the scene of mortal combat whereon the struggle is played out to its decisive end to determine the future destiny of the Roman race and of the Mother City of Rome.

---

[1] Von Duhn, *Italische Gräberkunde*, Erster Teil, 1924, pp. 30-2.
[2] Von Duhn, *ibid.*, p. 301 sq.; Åberg, *Bronzezeitliche und Früheisenzeitliche Chronologie*, Teil I, Italien, 1930, pp. 208, 217.

CHAPTER I

THE TROJAN LANDING AND TROIA NOVA

ipse humili designat moenia fossa
moliturque locum, primasque in litore sedes
castrorum in morem pinnis atque aggere cingit.[1]

THE tradition most generally accepted by historians of Rome who wrote prior to the publication of the *Aeneid*[2] tells how the Trojans, on reaching Latium, put in along a shore called Laurentum, not far from the mouth of the Tiber. The various accounts of the tradition, which is found even in Cato and Varro, differ in no important respect, and Dionysius of Halicarnassus may be made the mouthpiece for the rest: Τρῶες οἱ σὺν Αἰνείᾳ διαφυγόντες ἐξ Ἰλίου τῆς πόλεως ἁλούσης, κατέσχον εἰς Λωρεντόν, αἰγιαλὸν Ἀβοριγίνων ἐπὶ τῷ Τυρρηνικῷ πελάγει κείμενον, οὐ πρόσω τῶν ἐκβολῶν τοῦ Τεβέριος: 'The Trojans, fleeing with Aeneas from Ilion after its fall, landed at Laurentum, a shore of the Aborigines lying on the Tyrrhenian coast, not far from the mouth of the Tiber.' Dio Cassius adds that the disembarkation took place at the river Numicus which, as is shown in a later chapter, was that river now called the Rio Torto, which crosses the Campagna a few miles to the north of Ardea, and flows on to the Latian shore some sixteen miles south of the Tiber. It follows then that here was the tract of coastland known as Laurentum, and here the Trojans were thought to have ended their long wanderings.[3]

The historians are also in agreement that Aeneas' first task was to build a camp, and that the place where it was pitched was called Troia. Some writers suggest that it was so named before the coming of Aeneas, others that it received the name from the Trojans. All, however, is in the dim region of myth, fabricated probably in explanation of the existence of this

---

[1] *Aen.*, VII, 157-9.
[2] Livy, I, 1; Dio Cassius, *Is. Tzetz. ad Lycoph.*, 1232 (followed by Zonaras, VII, 1); Strabo, V, 229, Dion. Hal., *A.R.*, I, 45 and 63; Varro, *apud Servium, Ad Aen.*, IX, 8; Cato, *Or., apud Servium, Ad Aen.*, I, 5; Servius, *Ad Aen.*, I, 5, VII, 31, 158; IX, 8, 236. This tradition is also recorded by Appian, I, 1.
[3] The whole question is discussed at length by H. Boas, *Aeneas' Arrival in Latium, Allard Pierson Stichting, Archaeologisch-Historische Bydragen*, VI, 1938, p. 53 sq.

place-name on the Latian shore. 'Troy', in Latin *Troia*,[1] which is found in many places, including not only Latium and elsewhere in Italy, but also in Asia Minor and even farther afield, is considered by scholars to be pre-Latin and to be connected with *troare*, derived from a root indicating the movement of passing to and fro, as Klausen first pointed out.[2] Knight, in his recent interpretation of the name, takes it to signify a maze and then a place where there is a maze, or where a maze-dance was ritually performed,[3] making an apt comparison with the *Truia* or *Ludus Troianus*,[4] the military ride performed by young Roman nobles and mentioned in the *Aeneid*.[5] The character, however, of the coastal district of Latium, essentially grazing land, well fits the appellation of 'pasture', a place where cattle describe mazy wanderings as they graze, and is one which may go back to an early age when clearings in the forest belt were remarkable as pastures.

The records leave no doubt that a place called Troia existed near the mouth of the Numicus,[6] and give the added information that traces of some kind of settlement were to be seen there. A local legend which Dionysius learned from the inhabitants of the district accounted for the presence of two altars at this landing-place. They told how, when the Trojans first came to shore, they suffered from thirst, for there was no water in the place. Then springs of sweet water welled up from the ground of their own accord and all the army was watered. The two altars, one facing east, and the other west, and called Τρωικὰ ἱδρύματα, marked the place where Aeneas made a thank-offering for the water.[7] Ruins of some kind were to be seen there even in the second century A.D. which were connected with the Trojan landing, for Appian[8] writes as

[1] Mentioned by ancient commentators: Varro, *L.L.*, V, 18; Festus, *sub voce 'Troia'*, p. 367 M, 504, Lindsay.

[2] Klausen, *Aeneas und die Penaten*, 1839-40, II, pp. 822, 831; followed by Carcopino, *V.O.O.*, 1919, p. 405 sq. and especially p. 407, note 1, where there is a full philological discussion; also Frank, *A.J.P.*, XLV, 1924.

[3] W. F. J. Knight, *Cumaean Gates*, 1936, p. 107 sq.

[4] Knight, *ibid.*, p. 76.

[5] *Aen.*, V, 545-603.

[6] Cicero's *praedium Troianum* may have been in this coastal district, especially if the disputed reading could be taken as *Lavinium* and not *Lanuvium*: *Ad Atticum*, IX, 9, 4, and 13, 6.

[7] Dion. Hal., *A.R.*, I, 55.

[8] Appian, I, 1; cf. Servius, *Ad Aen.*, VII, 31: *in Laurolavinio castra fecit cuius vestigia adhuc videntur*. This may, however, refer to Lavinium.

PLATE 5. View of the site of Ostia from across the Tiber, looking upstream
(see page 4)

PLATE 6. Tor Bovacciana (see page 7)

PLATE 7.   Foundations of the eastern gate of
the *castrum* (see page 16)

PLATE 8. Portion of the *castrum* wall, showing characteristic tufa (see page 17)

if he saw them for himself: ἔνθα καὶ στρατόπεδον αὐτοῦ δείκνυται, καὶ τὴν ἀκτὴν ἀπ᾽ ἐκείνου Τροίαν καλοῦσιν: 'there, too, his [Aeneas'] camp is shown, and they call the shore Troia after him'.

This tradition of a landing on the Laurentian shore which prevailed before the *Aeneid* was written and which is so well accredited by the classical sources, must in its nature be very ancient, for its origin is clearly to be sought in times prior to the founding and development of Ostia, the port of Rome at the mouth of the Tiber. It reflects those early ages in the history of Latium, perhaps as far back as the eighth and seventh centuries B.C., when trade from overseas was brisk all along the coast as far as the northern cities of Etruria. Merchants may have put in with their wares on the shore of Latium where the outlets of the rivers with their quiet sandy beaches and wide lagoons could have given safe harbourage for purposes of barter and trade.[1]

For Vergil, however, the Trojans first come to land in Italy on the banks of the Tiber. After passing the coast of Latium at early dawn emblazoned with fair colours, and in calm of wind and wave, they sight a grove at the water's edge, through which the river flows to the sea in swirling eddies of yellow sand, and where many song-birds flit over the water, or fly through the grove:

> *hunc inter fluvio Tiberinus amoeno*
> *verticibus rapidis et multa flavus harena*
> *in mare prorumpit. variae circumque supraque*
> *adsuetae ripis volucres et fluminis alveo*
> *aethera mulcebant cantu lucoque volabant.*[2]

Here Aeneas bids the crews turn the prows to land, and the fleet is beached on the river bank. A feast is then spread on the sward beneath the trees, and platters of spelt are served for dishes. When the Trojans in hunger eat these rough cakes, the prophecy of 'eating their tables'[3] is brought to fulfilment, and Aeneas recognizes the promised land.

In bringing the Trojans to land on the banks of the Tiber, it seems that Vergil must have wished to do poetic honour not only to the river that runs by Rome and links her with the sea, but also to a place which he envisaged as worthy of a legendary

---

[1] Frank, *Economic History of Rome*, 1927, p. 46.   [2] *Aen.*, VII, 30-5.
[3] *Aen.*, III, 253-7.

setting in this, to a Roman of his time, legend of all legends, to a place significant both in history and in the reality of his day, and of increasing importance in his own age, that is, to the port of Ostia.

The attempt, however, to locate Aeneas' landing-place as visualized by Vergil, must be based on a consideration of the topography of the river as it was known to the poet. At that time[1] the mouth was in several respects greatly different from what appears to-day. Through long ages the Tiber has brought down in its course vast quantities of alluvial material which is deposited at the mouth. (It has been calculated that the river carries down yearly four to five million cubic metres of solid matter eroded from the friable rock over which it flows for the most part of its course.) Servius states that the Tiber was called by the Romans 'Serra' and 'Tarentum' because such a great amount of erosion took place.[2] The great plain which stretches from the low hills of Dragoncello to Palidoro and Tor Paterno has been built up from these alluvial deposits. The process has gone on rapidly through all the ages, and in the last centuries has become even more rapid. Now the actual mouth is roughly three miles away from the nearest ruins of Ostia, and these, at the beginning of the third century A.D. lay on the edge of the shore.[3] The material which is debouched into the sea cannot readily be carried away because the current along that part of the coast runs from south to north; on the south, however, in the region of the Canale dello Stagno, the coast has only advanced six hundred feet since Roman times. The accompanying map indicates the approximate coastline in the Augustan age (fig. 2).

The extension of the coastline, however, is not the only change which has taken place. Since the time of Trajan the Tiber, near its mouth, has been divided into two streams, which flow one on each side of the Isola Sacra. The southern arm, now called Fiumara, is the natural stream, the one, that is, up which the Trojans sailed; the other, on which the small port

---

[1] The substance of this paragraph is taken from Carcopino, *V.O.O.*, 1919, p. 497 sq., and Ashby, *J.R.S.*, 1912, p. 192 sq.

[2] Servius, *Ad Aen.*, VIII, 63: *quasi ripas ruminans et exedens.* 'Tarentum' is probably derived from *tero.*

[3] Torre S. Michele, built on the shore by Pius V in 1568, now stands a mile distant from the mouth. From this perhaps can be calculated the rate at which the silting up is taking place, though it must not be assumed that the rate is uniform.

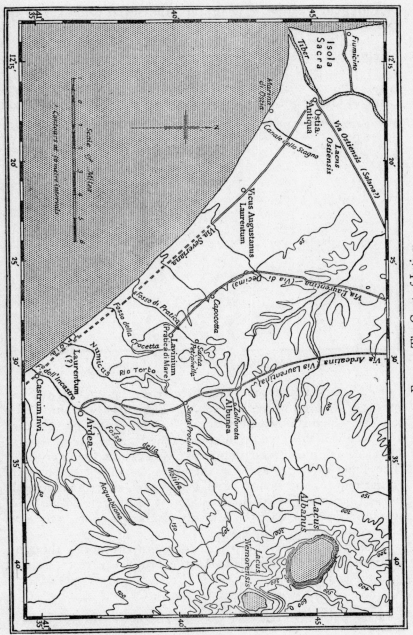

Fig. 1. The Coast of Latium.

of Fiumicino stands, is in origin an artificial canal cut in the times of Claudius and Trajan when the Portus was built.[1]

The direction of the river's course immediately Ostia is reached has suffered a change. As is seen in the map, prior to 1557 there was a wide curve in the form of an ox-bow, by which the river meandered round to flow past the mediaeval castle of Ostia, but in September of that year a disastrous flood

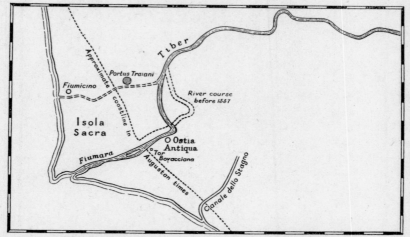

FIG. 2. The mouth of the Tiber in Augustan times.[2]

caused the water to cut a channel across the neck of the last meander before the sea is reached. The curve was thus left a dry bed which is now called Fiume Morto. At the present day, as a result of this change in course, the warehouses of ancient Ostia, which once stood along the riverside, are being eroded.[3] The Tiber as Vergil knew it, therefore, ran in one stream only to the mouth, and before flowing by Ostia, described a deeply curved meander, so rounded as almost to encircle an island in its course; and Ostia lay practically on the sea-shore, very near the actual mouth of the river.

If one would see the place where, in the poet's thought, Aeneas and the Trojans turned the prows upstream on that

[1] Ashby, *J.R.S.*, 1912, p. 192 sq.
[2] After an anonymous map of 1557, and Carcopino, *V.O.O.*, 1919, p. 501, fig. 24; and planche xv.
[3] In the excavations of 1938 efforts were being made to arrest the damage done by erosion.

prophetic dawn of day, he should go down to Ostia, and passing through the ruins to their outermost limit, stand upon the modern bridge which spans the river and carries the road across from the Isola Sacra to the modern Ostiense. Just here, perhaps, is the point where sea and river met in Vergil's day. Now to the westward the water passes on its course for almost another three miles, fringed with low shrubs and herbage and traversing level fields. On the east lie the ruins of Ostia low on the river bank, where the Trojans in their gliding ships found, instead of the busy port of Vergil's day, greensward for their resting place (pl. 5) Near the bridge, and on the left bank of the river, is a crumbling tower of the tenth century, Tor Bovacciana (pl. 6), standing now without significance but once marking the river's mouth, neglected, and incorporated in a mean dwelling house. As such it was seen by Richard Cœur de Lion once when he disembarked at the mouth: '[rex] intravit Tyberim ad cuius introitum est turris pulc[h]errima sed solitaria'.[1] This tower is built on the foundations of a square building of Roman times, which may have been, according to Carcopino,[2] a tomb or a lighthouse. If one may accept the latter more attractive suggestion, it is worthy of note that its situation in Roman times must have been on the very verge of river and sea; from here its light, easily visible to north and south along the low-lying coast of Latium, may well have marked for oncoming vessels the entrance to the harbour of Ostia.

The epic landing of the Aeneadae took place at dawn of day when sea and sky were flushed with hues of rose and saffron. When they were yet on the open water a calm befell them. At this moment of quiet expectancy, in the fair colours of that glorious dawning, Aeneas looked forth from the ship and beheld a mighty grove:

> atque hic Aeneas ingentem ex aequore lucum
> prospicit.[3]

Amid the grove and in its shade flowed the Tiber to join the sea.

---

[1] *Mon. Germ. SS.*, XXVII, p. 114; *apud* Paschetto, *Ostia colonia romana*, p. 102; Vaglieri, *Ostia*, p. 107. It has been calculated by Carcopino that the actual mouth in Augustan times was about 340 metres to the east of this tower. *V.O.O.*, 1919, p. 500, note 1, and following pages.

[2] *Ibid.*, p. 500, note 1.

[3] *Aen.*, VII, 29-30.

At the present day the country in the immediate neighbour-hood of Ostia is devoid of trees, but there is every probability that the maritime forest growth indigenous to the west coast of Italy[1] grew all along the shore by the Tiber's mouth in the poet's day, and covered the few hundred metres which lay between the sea and the docks of Ostia. There is no reason to suppose that the forest would be cleared from the shore, even when Ostia increased in importance, because the closely grow-ing trees and the umbrella pines with their branching tops would afford some degree of shelter from the sea winds, and their roots would knit together the sand of the dunes and pre-vent its being blown inland. As close to the Tiber as Castel Fusano a belt of forest still grows in all its primeval luxuriance, and such might well be the natural setting for Vergil in which the Trojans first entered the river of the land assigned to them by sure prophesy. The whole scene, however, takes on the grandeur of epic colouring, it becomes more lovely than nature ever made it, and under the poet's transcendent touch the primeval wood becomes an ordered grove musical with singing birds, and possessed of quiet shade, and the winds about it miraculously die down.[2]

After sending out scouts to prospect the land, and hearing that it is that of the Latins, Aeneas sends an envoy to the city of the king. Then he proceeds to build a settlement for the safety of all until he shall have founded the promised city of Lavinium. He himself chooses the place for this, their first abode on Italian soil, marks the line of the walls with a shallow ditch, and surrounds it with a rampart and battlements:

ipse humili designat moenia fossa
moliturque locum, primasque in litore sedes
castrorum in morem pinnis atque aggere cingit.[3]

This founding is after the manner of a camp, strongly fortified, a place of defence to harbour the Trojans until Aeneas' mission in Italy is fulfilled. The fleet was moored to the grassy verge of the bank when first they landed:

[1] For a description of the forest, see Introduction, p. xii.
[2] H. Boas, *Aeneas' Arrival in Latium, Allard Pierson Stichting, Archaeologisch-Historische Bydragen*, VI, 1938, p. 59 sq., discusses the question of the pleasant descrip-tion of the Tiber's mouth, and suggests that it is in accordance with the Alexandrine view of Nature.
[3] *Aen.*, VII, 157-9.

cum Laomedontia pubes
gramineo ripae religavit ab aggere classem.[1]

Later perhaps it was enclosed on the landward side by a rampart of earth:

classem, quae lateri castrorum adiuncta latebat,
aggeribus saeptam circum et fluvialibus undis
invadit.[2]

So Carcopino interprets this passage;[3] yet on this point doubt may well be felt as to whether the fleet was really enclosed within fortifications, and whether the reference in this passage is merely to the walls of the camp.

Carcopino makes much of this point, remarking on the difference between Aeneas' *castra navalia* and that of the Achaeans in the *Iliad* on the one hand, and on the other that of the especially Roman stratagem of enclosing camp and fleet within one stockade, practised by Scipio Africanus in 204 B.C., and by Caesar during the second invasion of Britain.[4] Perhaps this question should not be pushed too far, for a desire to pursue it to a logical conclusion only results in the loss of poetic appreciation and of dramatic situation. We are in an atmosphere of magical epic, where Cybele can later work her wonders to succour the Trojan cause,[5] for when Turnus, attacking the camp during Aeneas' absence, purposes to set fire to the fleet drawn up on the bank of the Tiber, the ships, magically transformed into sea-nymphs, plunge into the river, and swim away. Ships which obey the command of an enchantress's metamorphosis need not be confined within a Caesar's prosaic ramparts.

A good deal can be learnt from the *Aeneid* as to the situation of Aeneas' city-camp. Clearly it lies not far from the shore, for it can be seen from the sea. When Aeneas is returning from seeking Etruscan alliance and support, he descries the camp from the ship's high bows, and flashes a signal to the Trojans.

Iamque in conspectu Teucros habet et sua castra,
stans celsa in puppi, clipeum cum deinde sinistra
extulit ardentem. clamorem ad sidera tollunt
Dardanidae e muris.[6]

---

[1] *Aen.*, VII, 105-6.   [2] *Aen.*, IX, 69-71.   [3] Carcopino, *V.O.O.*, 1919, pp. 515-16.
[4] Livy, XXIX, 35, 13-14; Caes., *De Bell. Gall.*, V, 11, 4-5.
[5] *Aen.*, IX, 107-22; X, 215-35.   [6] *Aen.*, X, 260-3.

Furthermore, one of the gates is described as being very close to the sea:

> *locum insidiis conspeximus ipsi,*
> *qui patet in bivio portae quae proxima ponto.*[1]

On the other hand the camp on one side gave immediately on to the Tiber; so much so that when Turnus was surrounded within its walls, and hard-pressed by the Trojans, he escaped by throwing himself fully armed into the river and safely rejoined his comrades:

> *tum demum praeceps saltu sese omnibus armis*
> *in fluvium dedit.*[2]

Thus it appears from the action of events that Aeneas' camp was so situated as to be within sight of the sea and yet on the river bank; it cannot thus have been far from the mouth.

In the ninth book of the *Aeneid*, in the account of the attack made on the camp during Aeneas' absence in quest of help from Evander, is a clear statement that one side of it was bounded by the Tiber. After Nisus and Euryalus have been slain, their severed heads are paraded before the cheering Rutuli, but the Trojans look upon such a spectacle with horror. They front the Rutulian line along the left side of the camp; *on the left*, because the right side is girded by the river.

> *Aeneadae duri murorum in parte sinistra*
> *opposuere aciem (nam dextera cingitur amni.)*[3]

Scholars have been at pains to discover from these lines what was the form of Troia Nova, for they seem to imply that it had only two sides. As Heyne[4] pointed out, the orientation also appears to be mistaken, in that the enemy advances from the south, and the camp must therefore face towards the land. Bonstetten[5] found a solution which is acceptable to Carcopino[6] because it depends on a location near the last curve of the river's course: 'Un camp fait toujours face au point d'attaque. Enée

[1] *Aen.*, IX, 237-8. Carcopino, *V.O.O.*, 1919, p. 517, would argue from the use of the superlative that there were at least three gates.
[2] *Aen.*, IX, 815-16.
[3] *Aen.*, IX, 468-9; cf. *Aen.*, IX, 790: *partem quae cingitur unda.*
[4] Heyne,[4] III, pp. 414-15.
[5] Bonstetten, *Voyage dans le Latium*, 1805, p. 80.
[6] Carcopino, *V.O.O.*, 1919, pp. 518-19.

qui était défendu à peu près sur trois côtés avait tourné son
camp au sud-ouest, un peu vers la mer, et avait, dès lors, le
fleuve à sa droite. Mais pourquoi le point d'attaque est-il à la
gauche du camp et non du côté de la mer? C'est que le fleuve,
en se courbant, venait couvrir une partie du front de l'armée
troyenne.' In view of the archaeological knowledge possible
in the early nineteenth century when Bonstetten travelled and
wrote, such a conclusion is not unreasonable; neither is it so
for Carcopino who formed his theory before the excavations
at Ostia apposite to this inquiry had been carried out. The last
curve of the river has little or no relation to, or influence on,
the site of Troia Nova.[1] As in the case of the *castra navalia*,
the question of plan must not be pushed too far, for often in the
sphere of poetry material details intrude only to spoil. Perhaps
the interpretation offered by Heinze[2] of these difficult lines
may be accepted: Vergil in thought followed the Tiber down
from Rome and consequently placed the camp from the point
of view of the seaward course of the river; thus to one looking
downstream the river would be on the right, and the battle-line
on the left. From this visual aspect Vergil was identifying himself in thought with Aeneas, *pater* Aeneas, who at this time was
absent seeking help from Evander who dwelt on the Palatine
Hill, on the site, that is, of future Rome; his young warrior son
and faithful companions would be all the while the object of
his solicitude until he could rejoin them. That is perhaps as
far as our interpretation should be permitted to go, and it is
one naturally appreciable to the poet's own contemporaries,
whose viewpoint would be from Rome, and has a humanistic
reference to the great figure-head of the poem.

In several passages[3] in the *Aeneid* the city-camp is clearly
called by its name; the epithet *nascens* occurring in two of them
leaves no possible doubt that the reference is to Aeneas' settlement on the Tiber, and not to Phrygian Troy. Especially
noticeable is the incident when the youthful Iulus performs his
first exploit in war by slaying Numanus with his bow: Apollo,
watching from on high, commends him and his posterity with
the words:

---

[1] See below, p. 16 sq.
[2] Heinze, *Virgils epische Technik*, 1908[2], pp. 350-1; quoted by Carcopino, *V.O.O.*,
1919, p. 519.
[3] *Aen.*, VII, 233; X, 27, 74, 214.

'macte nova virtute, puer, sic itur ad astra,
dis genite et geniture deos. iure omnia bella
gente sub Assaraci fato ventura resident,
nec te Troia capit.'[1]

'Troy is not great enough for thee.' The first settlement on Italian soil is a tyro's training ground to try his youthful skill; in time will come a greater sphere for his prowess; and although Rome was to be greater than even Phrygian Troy, yet it is in the *new* Troy where his valour is put to the test, in the newly attained land of prophetic promise. Thus indirectly is brought into connection with the first Trojan settlement on Italian soil the future greatness of the Julian family, the *Gens Iulia.*

It is clearly stated, then, that the newly-built camp, called Troia, a reincarnation of that fatal Troy which they have left in Phrygia, is so situated as to be bounded by the Tiber on one hand, and to be visible from the sea. As Servius remarks, there is only one place which could correspond with such a site, and that is somewhere in Ostian territory: 'apparet . . . castra Troiana in Ostiensi fuisse, si quidem nullus alter locus in Laurolavinati hinc fluvio cohaeret, hinc pelago'.[2]

It is clear then that Vergil visualized the landing of Aeneas as taking place on the river bank where in his own day Ostia was to be seen. A consideration of the walk round the site of Rome in the eighth book of the *Aeneid*[3] will convince the reader of the poet's power of thinking away existing monuments, and of imagining primeval grass-covered slopes where the cattle lowed and grazed. So perhaps he thought of the Tiber fringed with the forest growth, of the peaceful flowing water, and the green banks, and perhaps in phantasy brought the Trojans home to a spot round which legend had in his own time gathered, to some place sacred from antiquity where Aeneas might first have paid homage to the gods of the new land. An inquiry into the Republican and Augustan remains discovered at Ostia and of the early origins of the place, throws light both on the poet's intent, and on the scene before his mind when he wrote.

[1] *Aen.*, IX, 641-4.
[2] Servius, *Ad Aen.*, IX, 236; cf. *Ad Aen.*, VII, 31: *circa Ostiam ubi prima Aeneas castra constituit.*
[3] *Aen.*, VIII, 337 sq.

Carcopino[1] considered that Troia Nova was to be recognized in the place where traces of the earliest settlements were found, near the bend of the river which after the floods of 1557 became the Fiume Morto.[2] He based his conclusion, however, chiefly on an impossible derivation of the name of Ancus Martius, the mythical founder of Ostia, from ἀγκών, signifying the bend in the course of the river. These conclusions are now no longer tenable in view of the discoveries which have been made by excavation since they were published.

In ancient[3] as in modern times harbourage along the whole of the western coast between Spezia and Gaeta has never been very good. Even now Civitavécchia is the only harbour of any consequence to be found along all this stretch of coast-line. There was none safe for large ships, and the two which served the flourishing Etruscan maritime commerce of the seventh century, Graviscae and Pyrgi, the ports respectively of Tarquinii and Caere, were little more than roadsteads. It is not known for certain whether the Tiber mouth had any part in the earliest trading activity, and tradition ascribed the beginnings of Ostia to a later date, regarding as founder the mythical king of Rome, Ancus Martius.[4] Livy's notice indicates the industry associated with its origin: 'in ore Tiberis Ostia urbs condita, salinae circa factae'.[5] Thus, since the record of the founding implies that the new city was connected with the working of salt-beds, perhaps it was the presence of these, rather than a roadstead or harbourage at the mouth of the Tiber, which caused some early settlement to come into being. These salt-beds are known to have existed from prehistoric times until about sixty years ago when the lacus Ostiensis was drained. After the Romans gained domination of the Etruscan cities on the right bank, they were superseded in importance by those of the Silva Moesia.[6] The antiquity of the Via Salaria, i.e. the 'Salt Road', perhaps is proof of that of the salt-beds near Ostia, for it was reputed to be the oldest Roman road, and may have received such a name because it was the route by which salt from the beds on the left bank of the Tiber could be procured.[7]

[1] Carcopino, *V.O.O.*, 1919, pp. 523-5.   [2] See above, p. 6 and fig. 2.
[3] This account is based on that of Ashby, *J.R.S.*, 1912, 153 sq.
[4] Blakeway, *J.R.S.*, XXV, p. 129 sq., shows that Rome may first have been Hellenized by the Tiber route.
[5] Livy, I, 33, 9.   [6] Ashby, *J.R.S.*, 1912, 153 sq.
[7] Ashby, *Classical Topography of the Roman Campagna*, I, 1902, p. 128.

The traditional date of the founding of Ostia in the time of the kings has not been substantiated by archaeology, since nothing has been found belonging to an epoch earlier than that of the end of the fourth century B.C. On the other hand there may have been an earlier settlement, as Ashby[1] suggests, nearer Rome, on the other side of the marshes, which was the forerunner of Ostia proper. Her primitive origin, however, must be sought in the necessity for guarding the mouth of the Tiber when the power of Rome was being asserted over the neighbouring Latin communities.[2] The stages in this early development cannot now be traced, but it must be later than the destruction of Ficana, which was situated higher up the river on the left bank, and earlier, for instance, than the fall of Veii, which held a dominant position near the right bank, and at the time of her *floruit* must have been powerful enough to have control of the Tiber and its crossings both to the east and west of Rome. If the primary purpose of Ostia proper was to defend the coast of Latium, this was soon outgrown, for the expansion of Ostia[3] as an important harbour was intensified with the earliest beginnings of Rome's power on the sea, and with the inauguration of the fleet during the first Punic war. In 267 B.C. four *quaestores classici* were instituted, one being assigned to Ostia.[4] It follows that Ostia must at that date have already been for some time in existence, and that the actual foundation can consequently be put back as far as the last decade of the fourth century,[5] a date which is in accord with archaeological discoveries. During the second Punic war Livy[6] refers to Ostia as both a naval base and a harbour: he states that in 217 B.C. supplies for the Roman army, which was in Spain, were sent out from the port. Thenceforth historical references show that Ostia, in addition, became a storehouse for grain and thus played her part not only in the expansion of the naval, but also of the commercial, power of Rome.[7]

---

[1] Ashby, *J.R.S.*, 1912, 153 sq.

[2] Pais, *Storia Critica di Roma*, I, 1913², p. 470; De Sanctis, *Storia di Roma*, I, p. 383; Wilson, *Papers of the British School at Rome*, XIII, p. 42 sq.

[3] Most authorities agree on a date in the second half of the fourth century B.C.; Carcopino, *V.O.O.*, 1919, pp. 32-3, would assign the foundation to 325 B.C., following Vaglieri, *Boll. Comm.*, 1911. Calza, *Guida di Ostia*, p. 6, dates it to 335 B.C.

[4] Lydus, *De Mag.*, I, 27.

[5] In 278 B.C. a fleet from Carthage landed at Ostia.

[6] Livy, XXII, 37, 57.

[7] See Calza, *Guida di Ostia*, p. 6, for a summary of the history of Ostia.

PLATE 9. The western end of the *area sacra* showing in the background the platform of the shrines, and in the foreground remains of a colonnade (see page 21)

PLATE 10. The eastern end of the *area sacra* showing the fountain and well-head (see page 21)

PLATE 11. The enclosure in the *area sacra* sacred to
Jupiter Optimus Maximus (see page 23)

PLATE 12. Shrine with altar *in situ*, inscribed *Veneri sacrum* (see page 23)

The earliest archaeological remains found on the site of Ostia, those ranging from the late fourth to the late third century B.C., were discovered near the Via dei Sepolcri. They are the furniture of tombs built on the virgin sand comprising Campanian ware, fragments of carved bone, bronze mirrors, gold ornaments, and iron nails.[1] Perhaps to be related to these burials are the foundations of ovoid huts, probably of wattle and straw, found also on the virgin sand just inside the Sullan wall, associated with sherds of coarse ware worked by hand.[2] Nothing as yet has been found of an earlier date than the burial finds, and since the hut foundations lay almost alongside them, on the same level, separated only by the Sullan wall, the two appear to be contemporary. The inhabitants of these poor huts may have been humble workers of the salt-beds, or they may have been the first builders and workers of the naval base, but it is possible that the salt-workers' village may have been nearer the marshes, and that it still remains to be found.

The remains of the Republican buildings identified amongst, and distinguished from, those of Imperial times show that the main outlines of the plan of Ostia were laid down in the former period.[3] Such structures are the warehouses just inside the eastern gate, which in Republican times stood in the area of state-land, the boundary of which was marked by inscribed terminals. Three of these have been found; they are exactly alike, and bear the same inscription:

C. CANINIUS C. F. PRAETOR URBANUS DE
SEN[atus] SENTENTIA POPLI[com] IOUDICAVIT

and are not later than the age of Sulla. They are of particular interest as being the earliest inscriptions found at Ostia. The other Republican monuments are the city wall faced with small roughly hewn stones (*opus incertum*) of the age of Sulla, remains of a portico and columns of a soft volcanic stone known as tufa, on the side of the main street (*decumanus*), a temple, twenty feet square, opposite the theatre, the wet dock near the imperial palace of uncertain date because it is situated at a point rather far west,[4] and certain tombs lying beside the Via Ostiensis, the

[1] Vaglieri, *Boll. Comm.*, 1911; Carcopino, *V.O.O.*, 1919, pp. 14-15.
[2] Vaglieri, *ibid.*, p. 230.
[3] This paragraph contains a summary of Ashby, *J.R.S.*, 1912, p. 155 sq., and Vaglieri, *Boll. Comm.*, 1911, p. 225 sq., *Monumenti Repubblicani di Ostia*.
[4] This dock is the one which at the present day is being eroded by the river.

high road communicating with Rome. Thus in this age Ostia had already the necessities and characteristics of a dockyard and emporium in her warehouses and quays, and of a city in her enclosure wall, arterial roads, and temples. Remains of the Augustan age are scanty: they comprise a few tombs, an inscription commemorating a soldier of the sixth praetorian cohort, who had a public funeral and site for his tomb because he lost his life in extinguishing a fire; and originally the theatre, as can be recognized from blocks of tufa, still preserved in the lower courses on, and near, the *decumanus*.

It is so that Ostia was known to Vergil; so must he have seen it if ever he walked the straight and cobbled *decumanus*, and turned aside to see the Tiber flowing on its course to the sea, or perhaps witnessed the arrival of ships from other lands, and saw in phantasy the Trojan ships quietly rowing upstream to their landing. Yet none of the monuments described seems fitting to inspire a poet's fancy; not around these could the legends of the Trojan landing linger or increase. If the poet really observed antiquity, if he looked with an intuitive eye on the realities before him, then it may be that the wraith of a place more ancient than all the rest, and yet in the midst of them, perhaps unseen or misunderstood by many, caught his interest and caused him to envisage here the site of Troia Nova.

The *castrum*[1] revealed by excavation, lying in almost the centre of the city as it is now known, seems certainly to date from the earliest beginnings and perhaps to represent the nucleus of the naval base. The form of it is rectangular (fig. 3), and it is situated about two hundred metres away from the river bank and about four hundred metres away from the coast-line of Augustan times. It is pierced by means of four gates of the long corridor type with three bastions (figs. 3 and 4), and it is crossed by the main street which runs directly through the two main gates from east to west. The original foundations of these rest on the older pavement which was found at a depth of more than a foot below the line of the street of Imperial Ostia (pl. 7). The plan (fig. 3) indicates that enough remains of the walls and gates fully to justify the restoration. The *castrum*, bounded on the north by the Tiber,

[1] The following account is taken from T. Frank, *A.J.P.*, XLV, 1924, p. 64 sq.; also Calza, *Guida di Ostia*, p. 26.

and in Vergil's day by the sea on the west, that is, by two natural boundaries, was orientated east-north-east by west-south-west, and enclosed by walls of tufa blocks, with special characteristics whereby their origin can be located.

These walls are of tufa from Fidenae and although at the present time incorporated in later buildings, are easily distinguished by the colour, a deep murky red, and by the presence

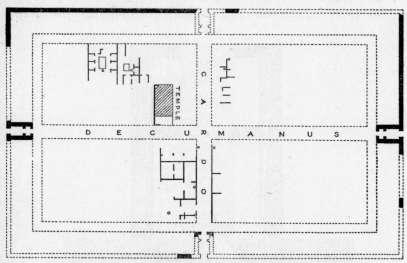

FIG. 3.   Plan of the *castrum*.

of large black *scoriae* (pl. 8), fragments of petrified charcoal indicating the volcanic nature of the stone. It has been thought that the use of this remarkable stone might afford grounds for the dating of the *castrum*. Tenney Frank's opinion that this tufa, found at Rome in the platform of the first Temple of Concord, built in 366 B.C., and in the post-Gallic wall of the Palatine Hill of approximately the same epoch, fell into disuse immediately afterwards, has lately been superseded. He would date the building of the *castrum* to the years following the fall of Fidenae in 426 B.C.,[1] that Latin town which constituted a barrier to the expansion of Roman influence eastward up the Tiber valley, situated as she was on an

[1] T. Frank, *A.J.P.*, XLV, 1924, p. 64 sq. His suggestion that the blocks used at Ostia were taken from the dismantled walls of Fidenae cannot now be credited; furthermore proof that Fidenae had walls is very slender; see *Ephemeris Dacoromana*, 1924, Fidenae.

eminence commanding the valley only a few miles from Rome herself.

In contravention of this dating, Säflund's[1] recent work on the Republican walls of Rome has shown that Fidenae tufa was used probably as late as 217 B.C. His discoveries would therefore cause the date of the *castrum* walls, to which he refers as Ostia I, to be put much later than Tenney Frank supposed. Säflund concludes that it cannot safely be calculated as much earlier than the second Punic war.[2] Further, he makes the

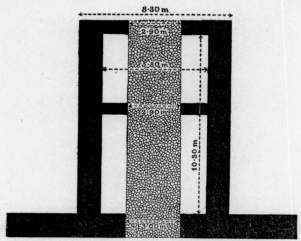

FIG. 4.   Plan of one of the *castrum gates*.

important suggestion that the first enclosure built at Ostia was not necessarily of hewn blocks of tufa (*opus quadratum*), but rather like the so-called Servian earthwork at Rome, probably a ditch and rampart against the earthen ramp of which the later stone wall was built. The construction of the *castrum* walls of Fidenae tufa may therefore find a place in the general defence works carried out against Hannibal in the second Punic war, but the actual date must still remain uncertain.[3] There is nothing to prevent the first beginnings in the form of an earthen wall being assigned to the earliest settlement of

[1] Säflund, *Le Mura di Roma Repubblicana*, 1932, p. 238 sq. I. A. Richmond, *J.R.S.*, 1932, p. 234 sq., in his review, does not altogether accept Säflund's conclusions.

[2] He considers that the Fidenae tufa to be seen on the Palatine Hill represents restoration work following the defeat at Trasimene.

[3] Calza, *N.S.*, 1914, p. 247, shows that Campanian ware associated with the wall gives a date between the end of the fourth and somewhere in the second century B.C.

Ostia proper in the late fourth century or even to an earlier salt-workers' encampment if the military form would allow this latter supposition. Thus Säflund's discoveries remove the discrepancy between T. Frank's date for the *castrum* and that of the earliest remains found on the site.

Calza[1] has pointed out that the side streets of the Imperial city preserve the lines of the ditches (*fossae*) since they follow along the rectangular lines of the fort, and thus the important fact emerges that the *castrum* is undoubtedly the original nucleus of the later city. Traces of buildings with tufa foundations, probably houses and shops, have been found within the enclosure, which appear to be contemporary with the walls, and indicate normal living activity within the *castrum*; these are indicated in the plan (fig 3). He points out, too, that the centre of the *castrum* lies in the Imperial forum, a space which from the earliest times was intersected by the two main streets of the lay-out of Ostia proper, the *decumanus* and the crossroad (*cardo*)[2] cutting it at right angles. It appears then that out of this humble origin grew the later thriving emporium, and that in subsequent building activities it was not entirely forgotten.

Uncertainty still remains as to whether all, or any part, of the *castrum* was free and exposed in the Augustan age. Tenney Frank thinks that Vergil could actually have seen the lines of the ditches, the walls, and the east, west, and south gates. As far as present research has gone, it is impossible to come to any safe conclusions regarding its appearance in the Augustan age, and doubt must yet remain as to whether Vergil could have seen enough to suspect here the presence of an older settlement in the typical form of a military camp with towered gateways and strong walls. The fact that Republican houses abut on the eastern side near the *decumanus* is very significant, suggesting that the walls were even then being incorporated in other buildings, and may have been entirely obscured in Vergil's time.[3] Yet it is quite reasonable to suppose that the gateways, which were of the long corridor type with three bastions (fig. 4 and pl. 7) continued to exist and to be visible right down to Imperial times, both those on the *cardo*

---

[1] Calza, *N.S.*, 1923; cf. Frank, *A.J.P.*, XLV, 1924, p. 65.

[2] Calza, *Ostia, Historical Guide to the Monuments*, 1924, p. 28.

[3] Wilson, *Papers of the British School at Rome*, XIII, p. 43, shows that the walls soon ceased to be defensive.

as well as those on the *decumanus*, all four well within the Sullan wall.[1] Their presence in the midst of the city, and in the heart of the busiest quarter, must have been remarkable. In this way perhaps a memory of the old settlement may have lingered, for to any thoughtful man they cannot have been without significance. Within the bounds of possibility may be the suggestion that this part of the city had a name, perhaps Castrum, Castra Troiana, or even Troia.[2] If any hint of the antiquity of this spot survived, either in visible appearance or in nomenclature, then tradition would in all likelihood gather round it, especially at a time when the Aeneas-cycle was becoming popularized. It may be that story had it that here the Trojans came home from the sea; if not in popular imagination, then perhaps in a poet's phantasy.

If in the time of Vergil the *castrum* at Ostia was to be seen, either in part or in entirety, the question arises as to whether the description of Aeneas' camp as given in the *Aeneid* can be found to correspond with it. Tenney Frank[3] considers that in many details the two are alike; Aeneas' camp was girt with ditches (*fossae*),[4] which according to him correspond to the ditches of the Ostian *castrum*; the fort is thought by Tenney Frank to have extended to the river and to have included the boats, agreeing with the appearance of the Ostian *castrum* in Vergil's time. In his opinion, archaeological evidence shows that the northern wall, that is the one facing the river, had disappeared to a very low level before Vergil's time, and may have been hidden in later structures. The gates in the *Aeneid* support towers,[5] and those that remain now were, according to Tenney Frank, strong enough to have done so.[6] It may certainly be admitted that the features of the Ostian *castrum* are not incompatible with the details in the *Aeneid*, yet the only safe conclusion is that the passage in the poem could be applied to any normal, or even abnormal, Roman camp, and that the poet envisaged a type rather than one in actual existence.

---

[1] Frank, *A.J.P.*, XLV, 1924, p. 65. They were repaired with harder stone in the second century B.C., as can be seen in the foundations of the bastions in their present state.

[2] For a discussion of the meaning of Troia, see above, p. 2 sq.

[3] Frank, *A.J.P.*, XLV, 1924, p. 65 sq.   [4] *Aen.*, IX, 314.

[5] *Aen.*, X, 121.

[6] Mr. C. A. Ralegh Radford has pointed out to the writer that no evidence exists at Ostia for towers over the gates, or for flanking towers.

PLATE 13. General view of Ardea from the north-west
(see page 31)

PLATE 14. View of the acropolis of Ardea from the west
(see page 31)

PLATE 16. View of the earthwork of Ardea from the western side
(see page 12)

PLATE 15. The western gateway
of Ardea (see page 31)

Another Republican monument on Ostian soil can be related to the epic landing of the Trojans. Facing the *decumanus*,
on the north side, and on the west of the theatre, is a piece of
ground, known as the *area sacra* (fig. 5, and pls. 9 and 10) the
sanctity of which appears always to have been respected, even
in subsequent building operations. Along the rear wall of this
enclosure, standing on a common platform, are the remains of

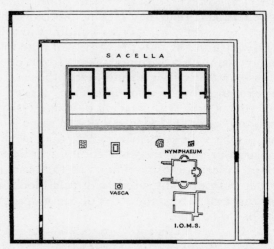

FIG. 5.   Plan of the *area sacra*, containing the four shrines, fountain,
and enclosure sacred to Jupiter Optimus Maximus.

four small temples, each with an altar before it on the ground
level: in the centre is a low well-head and on the east a fountain
(*nymphaeum*) and a walled space sacred to Jupiter (pl. 11).
Of all the Republican monuments[1] which could have been
known to Vergil, and thus perhaps have played a part in the
composition and in the action of the *Aeneid*, by far the most
significant is this sacred enclosure with its four shrines, filling
the space bounded (in the present state of the site) by the
house of Apuleius Marcellus, the Mithraeum, the theatre, and
the *decumanus*.

Excavation revealed three separate restorations in which the
original dimensions and orientation were carefully preserved,
and strata of votive pottery and coins pointing to a long period

[1] The account of this *area sacra* is taken from Paribeni, *M.A.*, vol. **XXIII**, p. 442 sq.

of unbroken worship. Underneath the platform were found, on the virgin sand, the primitive tufa walls of the first constructions, of a kind which could only have carried light upper courses of wood or crude brick or wattle. Under the second shrine was a tree trunk, and a great quantity of clay. These first shrines thus were humble and very poor, and it is not yet known whether the actual *area sacra* is contemporary with them. The fact, however, that their orientation follows the line of the *decumanus* and that they face it, indicates their importance. There are no remains of other buildings in the enclosure contemporary with these, and it is worthy of note that they did not originally stand on a common base. Overlaid on the remains of these first primitive shrines, were those of the second period. They stand now on a common base (*podium*) composed of blocks of yellow tufa, with a facing of lozenge-shaped stones (*opus reticulatum*) and a cornice, all of the same stone. They are all four of the simple form *in antis*, that is without any fronting pillars but only with walls ending in pilasters of tufa blocks; these have simple mouldings at the base, faced with stucco. Each is fronted by an altar of tufa blocks resting on the floor of the *area* before the steps of the *podium*, that is the raised floor of the shrine.

The *area* was originally surrounded on three sides by a portico and wall of *opus reticulatum*. In its first state it was open to the *decumanus* and entirely enclosed on the remaining sides. Paribeni considers that the portico served as a market, and that the enclosure remained free, and contained in early times in addition to the four shrines, only the altars and the well. It was, however, to undergo several changes before Vergil could have walked upon its ground.

Shops were subsequently built along the road, and the open end of the area was closed with a wall. Entries were made in the east and west sides, the internal portico destroyed, and shops and private houses added on the west side. A remarkable fact is that, although this *area sacra* became so closely hedged about with buildings connected with the commercial life of Ostia, yet it appears always to have been respected and its sanctity preserved. In Republican times two other sacred buildings were added within the precinct: the *nymphaeum* probably superseding in function the primitive well-head, and a second construction shown on the plan (fig. 5) lying to the

south-east. Its form is not quite regular, and it is not fairly
orientated with the other buildings in the *area*, or with the
decumanus. In each corner of the rectangular walls stands a
slab of travertine—a cream-coloured volcanic stone much used
by the Romans for building—inscribed i.o.m.s., and in the
centre of the floor are remains of a travertine column and
base (pl. 11).

The contents of five strata of votive offerings, chiefly pottery
and coins, found in close conjunction with the enclosure and
the shrines, give testimony of unbroken continuity of worship
from as early as the third century b.c. The building materials,
too, confirm this, belonging as they do to successive periods.
Although very few votive remains came to light which were
later than the age of Sulla, evidence of restoration gives a date
at least as late as the second century a.d. for the third rebuild-
ing of the shrines, and repairs to terracotta revetments and
plaster were done in the first century of the Empire. Thus the
continued building activity is significant,[1] pointing to the
continuance of the cults observed there, and unbroken venera-
tion for their sanctity.

There remains a question whether it is possible to identify
the four shrines, and to discover the deities to which they were
sacred. An inscription in the temple on the eastern side (pl. 12)
leaves no doubt that it was sacred to Venus for a marble altar
still stands on its original site, inscribed as being sacred to her,
veneri sacrum. The other three in themselves give not the
slenderest of clues, but it has been reasonably thought that an
inscription bearing the name of Publius Lucius Gamala, who
was, as his name indicates, a member of one of the leading
families of Ostia, may have reference to the shrines.[2] In it is
mentioned the building of four *aedes*, that is, temples, one of
which was sacred to Venus. 'P. Luc. Gamala constituit sua
pecunia aedes Veneris, Fortunae, Cereris, Spei.'[3] In another, P.
Lucilius is said to have restored them.[4] The Gamalae, however,
belong to the Imperial age, and it naturally follows that the
first inscription quoted cannot have reference to the original
building. If it refers to these shrines at all, it indicates some

[1] One *graffito* is important for this inquiry as it can be assigned with certainty to the
year 23 b.c., a date falling in Vergil's lifetime: *Caesare et Pisone cos pridie eidus.*
[2] Carcopino, *Mélanges de l'Ecole de Rome*, 1911, p. 193 sq.
[3] *C.I.L.*, XIV, 375.
[4] *C.I.L.*, XLV, 376.

subsequent restoration or repairs, as does the second inscription.[1] The deities of the shrines, for want of more convincing data, must naturally remain doubtful, but the occurrence of the name of Venus in this shrine (fig. 5), together with the inscription of Gamala, perhaps makes this identification at least very probable.

The nature of the building consecrated to Jupiter lying to the south-east of the *area* also must continue to be doubtful. The remains seem to indicate not so much a temple as a roofless shrine, as defined by Festus, 'Sacella dicuntur loca dis sacrata'.[2] It is perhaps a place marked off as sacred, in all probability where a thunderbolt fell:[3] or it might even, with more precision, be regarded as a *bidental*, a place, that is, where lightning had struck the earth and had been 'buried' by the expiatory offering of a two-year-old sheep known as a *bidens*. To Roman superstition such a spot always became taboo, and was regarded as consecrated to the god who had launched the bolt and wielded the lightning. Certainly the asymmetric orientation seems to be the outcome of some such chance circumstance, since even the line of the *decumanus* was not taken into account in the building of the shrine.

Turning off from the main street of the city, and entering through the enclosure wall, Vergil himself may have seen the four shrines in the state of their second restoration, standing on the *podium*, their walls and columns gleaming with white stucco, their roofs covered with revetments of terracotta, and the altars before the steps. An antiquarian as well as a poet, he must have recognized them as simple and holy places of the forefathers of his people. He may have seen, too, those walls, enclosing a spot where once the power of Jupiter was made manifest on earth. Such a place, so full of sanctity, so continuously revered in the midst of Ostia's commercial life, could not easily have been overlooked in the phantasy of a poet who divined and understood its humble antiquity.

If, in the description of Aeneas' camp in the *Aeneid*, an indirect reference may be seen to the *castrum* at Ostia, and if legend, in a traditionalizing age such as was that of Augustus,

---

[1] Carcopino, *Mélanges de l'Ecole de Rome*, 1911, p. 193 sq., has suggested that the house of Apuleius Marcellus belonged to the Gamalae, and that perhaps they made expiation for building on to the *area sacra*.

[2] Festus, *De V.S.*; Muller, p. 318.

[3] Livy, XXXII, 1, 10.

had grown around the memory of the primitive settlement on the river bank, nothing is more natural than that the early sanctuaries, whose worshippers lay buried in the graves along the *decumanus*, should also have had a part in the Aeneas-legend. Their antiquity may even have been exaggerated by tradition gathering round uninterrupted worship. In the *Aeneid* it is Jupiter who is closely associated with the events and portents which immediately follow the landing on the Tiber's bank. Aeneas, Iulus, and the Trojans recline under the branches of a tall tree. A feast is set before them and the food piled high on platters of spelt. All this, Vergil tells us, is at the express command of Jupiter:

sic Iuppiter ipse monebat.[1]

After the prophecy of the eating of the tables has been fulfilled, the Trojans pour libation to the god —

nunc pateras libate Iovi.[2]

Then Aeneas wreaths his brows with green leaves, and calls at this fateful moment upon the many deities who may attend this hour of destiny and the momentous future. Thereupon the almighty Father of heaven thunders thrice in a clear sky, and shows them a cloud flashing with rays of golden light, and the Trojans know that the day has come on which they are to found the walls commanded by fate.

hic pater omnipotens ter caelo clarus ab alto
intonuit, radiisque ardentem lucis et auro
ipse manu quatiens ostendit ab aethere nubem.
diditur hic subito Troiana per agmina rumor
advenisse diem quo debita moenia condant.[3]

These are the walls of the Trojan camp, that Troia Nova, which the gods ordained should arise in Italy, and should shelter Aeneas and his followers until their work should be done. As soon, then, as Jupiter's approval has been manifested, they renew the feast, in joy set up the great bowls of wine (*crateres*), and fill them to the brim. All these happenings

[1] *Aen.*, VII, 110.   [2] *Aen.*, VII, 133.
[3] *Aen.*, VII, 141-5. Mr. W. F. J. Knight has kindly brought to the writer's notice the remarkable sequence of eleven homodynes, beginning at l. 137: this stress pattern, where the accent falls at the beginning of the fourth foot in each line suggests the quick-moving excitement of one of the most impressive events in the *Aeneid*. (*Accentual Symmetry in Vergil*, p. 37.)

are under the high command and direct guidance of Jupiter. The god commands the eating of the tables, and with a great portent, 'omine magno',[1] of good fortune signifies his approbation of Aeneas. Why should this not have taken place, in the poet's mind, at that spot known to him at Ostia, which was kept sacred to Jupiter within that most ancient and sacred ground in the city? It was a spot, too, which appears not to have been a temple, but a shrine, where in all probability a thunderbolt had once fallen from heaven.

Lastly, if the shrines may be considered to be those referred to in the inscription of Gamala and thus may be identified as sacred to the four divinities, Venus, Fortune, Ceres and Hope, then some connection may be found with the Aeneas-legend. As has been shown, there is no doubt as to the shrine of Venus, and here we have to do with the divine mother of the good Aeneas, the founder of the Roman race. No deities were better able to attend him in the hazards of his destiny than Fortune and Hope. Perhaps the closest relation of all could be found between the shrine of Ceres, and the events which took place immediately after the landing on the banks of the Tiber. That meal, when the prophecy was fulfilled that they should in hunger eat their tables, was clearly of the nature of a sacramental meal. The whole event is momentous and solemn; the feast of fruits is heaped on platters of spelt at the command of Jupiter; the archaic word, *adorea*, and the sacrificial word, *liba*, add to the solemnity:

> *instituunt dapes et adorea liba per herbam*
> *subiciunt epulis (sic Iupiter ipse monebat)*
> *et Cereale solum pomis agrestibus augent.*[2]

The platters are spoken of as 'Cereale solum',[3] and at the moment when the prophecy is enacted, they are again described as 'exigua Ceres':

> *consumptis hic forte aliis, ut vertere morsus*
> *exiguam in Cererem penuria adegit edendi,*
> *et violare manu malisque audacibus orbem*
> *fatalis crusti, patulis nec parcere quadris:*
> *'heus, etiam mensas consumimus' inquit Iulus.*[4]

---

[1] *Aen.*, VII, 146.

[2] *Aen.*, VII, 109-11. Servius on line 109 defines *liba* as *placenta de farre, melle et oleo, sacris apta*.

[3] *Aen.*, VII, 111.   [4] *Aen.*, VII, 112-16.

The repetition of the name Ceres seems too insistent to be mere nomenclature, for the whole situation is determined by the fact that the platters of spelt (which was the ancient food of the Romans, and therefore constantly used in ritual), round, and divided into four quarters as was the Roman custom, were eaten by those for whom heaven had such a care.[1]

Several different interpretations of the ritual of the 'eating of the tables' (mensae) have so far found favour with scholars, of which two should be noticed. Klausen[2] considered that it was to be connected with the worship of the Penates, the Roman household gods, to whom offerings of spelt were regularly made. On the other hand Carcopino's[3] opinion was that the mensae were to be regarded as summanalia, cakes used in the worship of Summanus, a deity who was, according to him, the nocturnal counterpart of Vulcan (Volcanus). He was at pains to prove not only that this deity was the chief amongst those worshipped at Ostia, but also that a federal cult of Vulcan[4] existed on the site of Ostia before the foundation and development of the port. This explanation of the nature of the mensae would indeed well fit into the whole picture which he outlines of the early origins of Ostia and of the cults existent on her soil, yet Miss Boas[5] rightly points out the need for more convincing evidence both for the identification of Summanus with Vulcan, and for the assumption that summanalia necessarily means cakes offered in the ritual of Summanus. Of the two theories, that of Klausen seems the more appropriate, but needs review in the light of archaeological discovery made since his time. Rather have we some justification, according to present knowledge enriched by recent excavation, in seeing in the event as recounted in the Aeneid, a reference, veiled in Vergil's poetic manner, and yet lightly and brightly veiled, to the earliest sacred monuments of Ostia, and a hint of the great significance of Ostia as a grain port and granary. Miss Boas[6] makes the interesting suggestion that, by a stroke of artistry, Vergil may

[1] Cf. Aen., III, 257, and Servius' note on the shape of the cakes: ambesas, undique esas, hoc est rotundas.

[2] Aeneas und die Penaten, 2[e] Bde, 1839-40, pp. 680-90.

[3] V.O.O., 1919, p. 673 sq. On page 681 he quotes Festus, sub voce 'Summanalia', p. 349 M., 474; Lindsay: liba farinacea in modum rotae ficta.

[4] Carcopino, ibid., p. 39 sq.

[5] Aeneas' Arrival in Latium, Allard Pierson Stichting, Archaeologisch-Historische Bydragen, VI, 1938, p. 233. The question of the mensae is discussed at length, p. 221 sq.

[6] Boas, ibid., p. 234.

have found attractive the paradox that the Trojans suffered hunger where later there was to be abundance. For Vergil, too, the Trojans appease their hunger for the first time on Italian soil where shall arise the emporium which shall feed in later ages the great populace of Rome. That in the *area sacra*, and before those ancient shrines, one of them dedicated to the very goddess of the corn, a ceremony such as that of eating cakes of spelt was accustomed to be observed, and that at the sacramental feast tales were told of the Trojan landing, might be an attractive suggestion but without better evidence the mere suggestion would be indiscreet.

The ancient and sacred places of his country had a fascination both for Vergil the poet, as well as for Vergil the antiquarian. It is unlikely that the small and sacred ground at Ostia, so long revered, and still preserved in the reforms of Sulla and even in the trade of Augustan times, was overlooked by one who had so great an interest in the old sanctuaries. He may have known of the *castrum* close beside it, and so have thought that here, in his epic, the Trojans should come from the sea: here was the scene of their first communion with the gods of Italy, and here their first place of defence.

As has been seen,[1] in bringing the Trojans to land on the banks of the Tiber, Vergil broke away from a more widely prevailing tradition. The question arises as to why should Vergil thus make an innovation in departing from accepted popular and literary tradition? It may be that at Ostia local myths were growing up connecting the port with the Trojan landing and that, in a desire to bring the Tiber into the epic early, Vergil chose to accept them, or perhaps it was not the love of antiquity alone, but also a desire to do honour to the Julian house, and in particular to projects of Julius Caesar and Augustus for the expansion of Ostia which led him to set there the scene of the landing.[2] If this be so, then we have here in the *Aeneid* a good instance of Vergil's modernism of his solicitude for problems of his day and preoccupation with reality, and so the passage may be regarded as a plea for the betterment of existing conditions. Strabo,[3] writing in the Augustan

---

[1] See page 1 sq.
[2] The question is discussed at great length by Boas, *Aeneas' Arrival in Latium, Allard Pierson Stichting, Archaeologisch-Historiche Bydragen*, VI, 1938, p. 53 sq.
[3] Strabo, V, 231.

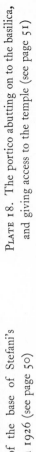

PLATE 18. The portico abutting on to the basilica, and giving access to the temple (see page 51)

PLATE 17. A corner of the base of Stefani's temple, excavated in 1926 (see page 50)

PLATE 19. View of Lavinium from the south-east (see page 54)

age, so describes the state of the Tiber's mouth as to indicate
that brisk trading could not well be carried on. He says that
it was silted up to such an extent that the heavy cargo boats
had to anchor far out in the surge, and that with peril to themselves, and that the merchandise had to be conveyed in smaller
boats up the river to Rome. Judging from this valuable contemporary account, the conclusion can be reached that the
function of Ostia in the time of Vergil was not so much that of
a harbour and port as of a receiving place and emporium for
overseas trade. The merchandise, in most cases grain, was
stored along the quayside until it was sold and transported to
Rome. It is known also that Augustus settled a colony of
veterans there.[1] As Carcopino aptly points out, the city seems
to have been almost entirely rebuilt under his reign.[2] The
theatre, for instance, was raised before 12 B.C. in one of the
consulships of Agrippa,[3] and Carcopino[4] considers that the
restorations carried out under P. Lucilius Gamala of the temple
of Vulcan, the four shrines and the road near the Forum, all
point to a definite programme of reconstruction, and indicate
the extent of the work done in Augustan times. He would even
go so far as to consider that Augustus had intended, and even
begun, to construct at Ostia the port of which Julius Caesar
had dreamed, but the evidence for this attractive suggestion is
perhaps too scanty to allow of insistence. In speaking of great
deeds done by mortal men which shall perish, Horace wrote the
lines:

> *sive receptus*
> *terra Neptunus classes Aquilonibus arcet,*
> *regis opus.*[5]

These are interpreted by one of the scholiasts as being a reference to projects under Augustus for the building of a port at
Ostia: 'divus Caesar duas instituerat res facere; portum Ostiensem munire'.[6] This passage, however, may have reference to
Julius Caesar rather than to Augustus, since it seems to be

---

[1] Pliny, *N.H.*, III, 56, and III, 46; also *C.I.L.*, XIV, 409, I, 10. It is doubtful
whether this inscription refers to the same colony since it belongs to the second century
A.D.
[2] *V.O.O.*, 1919, p. 729.   [3] *C.I.L.*, XIV, 82.   [4] *V.O.O.*, 1919, p. 730.
[5] Hor., *Ars Poet.*, 63-5.
[6] Porphyrion, *Ad Hor. Ars Poet.*, 63-4. It is referred by Acron, *ibid.*, to the *Portus
Lucrinus*.

founded on Plutarch's life of the former, in which a corresponding statement is found.[1] From this there seems little doubt that Julius turned his attention to the possibilities of Ostia as a port,[2] but the plans supposedly put forth by Augustus are at present without satisfactory evidence. Admittedly Vergil speaks of the landing-place on the Tiber's bank as a harbour (*portus*) in several passages, and whether this be a plea for the expansion of Ostia, and poetic championship in support of the emperor, or only a natural word for a natural and simple event, who shall say? In prophecy a promise is given the Trojans of safe harbourage on the Italian coast:

> *pauca tibi e multis, quo tutior hospita lustres*
> *aequora et Ausonio possis considere portu.*[3]

and perhaps we can leave them where their weary ships find rest:

> *immo, ubi defunctae finem portusque tenebunt*
> *Ausonios.*[4]

and seek no further into a mind and purpose which perhaps none now can ever fully understand.

---

[1] Plut. *Caes.*, 58; Suet., *Claud.*, 58.

[2] A notice in the *Chronica Minora*, I, p. 145 (ed. Mommsen), states: *navis Alexandrina primum in portu Romano introivit*. Carcopino, *V.O.O.*, 1919, p. 740, sees in this, proof that Augustus built a port at Ostia. It is, however, impossible to conclude satisfactorily what is the precise meaning of *primum* and of *Romano*.

[3] *Aen.*, III, 377-8; also III, 254, IV, 612-13, VII, 132, 201.

[4] *Aen.*, IX, 98-9.

CHAPTER II

ARDEA

locus Ardea quondam
dictus avis, et nunc magnum manet Ardea nomen,
sed fortuna fuit.[1]

ARDEA, the storied home of Turnus, lies westwards on the
Roman Campagna, four kilometres from the sea, and twenty-
three south of Rome, in a setting little different from that
which was seen in Augustan times. The surrounding pasture-
land, with here and there a sunken valley clothed with fresh
and verdant growth, and in the distance the deep blue of the
Mediterranean, brings to experience all that the poet may have
known, and is a fit prelude to the first view of the acropolis
(pls. 13 and 14) which dominates the fragrant fields. The
modern road from Rome, which follows in part the line of the
ancient Via Ardeatina, approaches the western side, and after a
sharp turn, leads up to the half-ruined mediaeval gateway (pl.
15). Here passes to and fro a constant succession of women and
children going down to the spring and the washing-tanks at
the foot of the slope some hundred yards away. Occasionally
a man on horseback passes through, and in the evening
gatherings of workers from the fields come in — stalwart girls
in simple peasant dress, full gathered skirt and cotton blouse,
bearing their hoes on their shoulders; sometimes a fisherman
is seen who has come barefoot from the shore to send his catch
to the Roman markets. Such is the life enacted before the
ancient citadel, in constant activity, and fulfilling the needs of
daily life unchanged since time immemorial.

On passing up the steep slope, and through the western
gate, the traveller is at once struck by the poverty of the
inhabitants and their dwellings: poor, ramshackle houses, roads
worn deep into the rock, rutted and unkept, a mediaeval palace
and a small Romanesque church with a Roman funerary altar
before it, all speak of the desolation of this most poetic place,
honoured in legend and myth and history, now peopled by only
two hundred poverty-stricken inhabitants, a mere wraith of
what it once has been. After traversing the plateau on which

[1] *Aen.*, VII, 411-13.

31

the city stands, the traveller comes to the eastern gateway, of
which little now is left, and will see on the north side of the gate
the ruined mediaeval tower and crumbling walls built out of
Roman stonework, and will look eastward over vineyard and
allotment to the outermost limits of the site and beyond, to
where in the distance the ranges of the Alban hills half enclose
the wide Campagna.

This Ardea, ruined and forgotten, hides within herself a
vanished greatness, for she bears the marks and characteristics

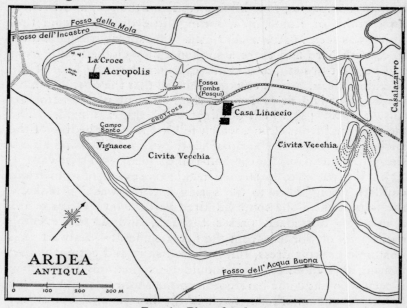

FIG. 6.   Plan of Ardea.[1]

of an ancient and independent Latin city with defence works
and communication with the sea.   The site (see the plan, fig. 6)
is bounded by the valleys of two streams, the Fosso della Mola
on the north and the Fosso dell' Acqua Buona on the south,
which converge below the city on the west to form the Fosso
dell' Incastro, a stream of considerable volume which reaches
the sea after about another four kilometres.   The natural
plateau of the acropolis stands about thirty metres above the
valleys, and is composed of the greenish-white tufa, characteristic of volcanic Latium, and of a greyish-yellow clay.[2]   On

[1] After Lindros, *B.M.*, April-July, 1934, pl. 1.   [2] Sestini, *B.M.*, April 1930, p. 8.

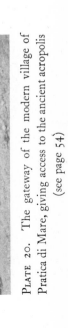

PLATE 21. The road from Pratica di Mare to the shore, looking towards the city (see page 57)

PLATE 20. The gateway of the modern village of Pratica di Mare, giving access to the ancient acropolis (see page 54)

PLATE 23.   The Fosso di Pratica (see page 68)

PLATE 22.   The Canale dello Stagno (see page 67)

the south and east sides of the acropolis there are remains of ancient fortification walls. The settlement was not confined to this area but extended to the south and east, landwards over the lower plateau of Civitavécchia and Casalazarro. The two latter regions are really geological extensions of the acropolis, and being bounded by the two rivers and the valleys, they are to some extent naturally fortified on the north and south. Separating them on the east, however, is a high earthwork and ditch pierced by a gateway, through which passes the line of the *decumanus*.[1] Archaeological finds have been made on the acropolis, in Vignacce and Civitavécchia and on the sides of the road outside the boundary of Casalazarro.

The flat rocky formation on which Ardea stands is one of several plateaux of tufa on the last seaward ridge of the Alban *massif*, and the site, characteristic of settlements originating in prehistoric times, on the Latian seaboard, is comparable with that of Lavinium,[2] Satricum (now Conca) and, in Etruscan territory, of Caere (Cerveteri) and Tarquinia (Corneto). They all stand some few miles inland, well raised above the coastline which in ancient times was swampy[3] and probably unhealthy, and well defended in the first place by nature; at the same time they have access to and from the sea by means of a nearby river and its valley which affords an easy means of communication.

The history of Ardea, such as can be gleaned from ancient writers, tells of a city of great antiquity,[4] once amongst the most flourishing in Latium, enjoying early independence and a modicum of wealth, but eventually coming to decline, and at last falling into a ruinous condition which would have caused even her name to have been forgotten had it not been for the sanctity of her ancient cults. Livy describes the Rutuli in the time of Tarquinius Superbus, as being 'gens ut in ea regione et ea aetate divitiis praepollens'.[5]

The tradition of maritime power, and of communication with the sea is borne out by the testimony of Polybius, who relates how Ardea was included in the first treaty between

---

[1] A second ridge bounding Casalazarro was long thought to be artificial, Richter, *A.I.*, 1884, pp. 102, 106, also Pasqui, *N.S.*, 1900, p. 60, but has been proved by Sestini, *B.M.*, 17, April 1930, to be natural.

[2] See below, p. 86 sq.   [3] See below, p. 114.   [4] Strabo, V, 228.

[5] Livy, I, 7; the tradition recorded in Livy, I, 5, 7, that Ardea was besieged by Tarquinius Superbus who desired plunder to distribute to his dissatisfied people, is another testimony of her comparative wealth at an early period.

D

Rome and Carthage as one of the five coastal towns of Latium which the Carthaginians were pledged not to molest.[1] According to his calculation the treaty belongs to the first year of the Republic, i.e. 505 or 507 B.C., a date which scholars have found no valid reason for rejecting.[2]

It appears, then, that at the end of the sixth century, Ardea was to some degree powerful by sea, and from it she must have drawn some of her wealth. This is the more significant when it is remembered that Antium, modern Anzio, the neighbouring port to the south, was held by the Volsci. Situated as she was, with easy access to the Alban hills, the harbour of Ardea must have served the Latin cities in the neighbourhood, both those farther inland on the plain, and those lying along the ranges.[3] Her earliest ways of communication were accordingly east and west. The line of the modern road to Lanúvio (Lanuvium) and the hills lies most probably on the line of a very ancient route connecting her with the inland cities.

Some ruins exist near the mouth of the Fosso dell' Incastro on the line of the ancient Via Severiana[4] which scholars have no hesitation in recognizing as those of the Castrum Invi, the port of Ardea. The writer has seen remains of late Republican times on the bank of the stream near the dunes, scanty, but enough to prove that the coast was not deserted in Vergil's age. The earlier existence of Castrum Invi is vouched for by references in Vergil, Ovid, Silius Italicus, and Martial.[5] The words of two of these writers are especially significant in that they couple the *Castrum* closely with Ardea: Silius Italicus says,

> *quos Castrum, Phrygibusque gravis quondam Ardea misit,*

and Martial,

> *Ardea solstitio castranaque rura petantur,*
> *quique Cleonaeo sidere fervet ager.*

[1] Polyb., III, 22: Καρχηδόνιοι δὲ μὴ ἀδικείτωσαν δῆμον 'Αρδεατῶν . . . Livy, XXI, 7, states that they were once powerful enough to join with the people of Zacynthus in colonizing Saguntum.

[2] H. Last, *C.A.H.*, vol. VII, p. 859. Beaumont, *J.R.S.*, 1939, p. 74 sq., has shown that a late sixth century date can be decisively confirmed, on the grounds especially that there is no mention of Spain.

[3] Boëthius, *B.M.*, June-July 1931, pp. 3-4.

[4] Nibby, *Analisi della Carta dei Dintorni di Roma*, vol. I, 1848[2], p. 440. Lanciani, *Wanderings in the Roman Campagna*, 1909, p. 312.

[5] *Aen.*, VI, 775; Ovid, *Met.*, XV, 726; Sil. It., VIII, 359; Martial, IV, 60, 1. Servius, *Ad Aen.*, VI, 768, confuses it with Castrum Novum, as does Rutilius, *Itin.*, 1, 232.

There can be little doubt that the Castrum Invi,[1] as its name implies, served in antiquity, not only as the port for Ardea, but also as a defence for the approach from the sea, a necessity perhaps in early days against marauding pirates. The shore is flat and sandy, with a gently shelving beach, which would allow safe and easy landing for ships.

It is interesting to see how Vergil knew of the tradition of a landing-place on this shore, and turned it to a dramatic purpose in the tenth book of the *Aeneid*.[2] Turnus is transported against his will from the midst of the fighting and taken by ship back to Ardea: with favouring wind and wave he is borne to the ancient city of his father Daunus:

> *labitur alta secans fluctuque aestuque secundo,*
> *et patris antiquam Dauni defertur ad urbem.*

A theory, which seems to have originated with Servius,[3] is that Invus was a god identical with Pan, and that this was a place sacred to him that afterwards became fortified. Nibby quotes the name of the Villa Priapi, mentioned as being in 'agro Ardeatino' in pontifical biographies of the tenth century A.D., in support of Servius.[4] In view, however, of the practical use which the *Castrum* served, and in which must surely be found its origin, this theory seems hardly acceptable.

In tracing the history of Ardea we find that she took a full share in the Latin leagues of the sixth and fifth centuries of which one such union is perhaps recorded in the inscription quoted in a fragment of Cato's *Origines*:[5] 'Lucum Dianium in nemore Aricino Egerius Laevius Tusculanus dedicavit dictator Latinus: hi populi communiter: Tusculanus, Aricinus, Lanuvinus, Laurens, Coranus, Tiburtis, Pometinus, Ardeatis Rutulus.' This is probably to be dated to the end of the sixth century.[6] These names represent all the really formidable opponents of Roman supremacy in Latium and the nucleus of the Latin alliance which Rome had to face in the early years of the fifth century. The list of thirty cities constituting a league

---

[1] The Fosso dell' Incastro is thought to preserve the name of the *Castrum*.

[2] *Aen.*, X, 687-8.

[3] *Ad Aen.*, VI, 768.

[4] Nibby, *Analisi della Carta dei Dintorni di Roma*, vol. I, 1848[2], p. 440; also Tomassetti, *La Campagna Romana*, 1910, II, 460-1.

[5] Cato, *Frag.*, 58P; cf. Festus, p. 128, L.

[6] The following account is taken from H. Last, *C.A.H.*, VII, p. 487; Boëthius, *B.M.*, June-July 1931, p. 7, accepts the dating.

directed against Rome as given by Dionysius[1] includes the name of the Ardeates, but most authorities do not accept the list as authentic.[2] Ardea, however, may have had her place in the treaty of Cassius, the *foedus Cassianum*, of 493 B.C.[3] At least we have the testimony from Cato's list of her standing among the neighbouring cities in the sixth century, and this time appears to mark her *floruit*: henceforward her prosperity declines and her name sinks into insignificance.

Events of the fifth century indicate the growing power of Rome, and the inability of the formerly independent Latin cities to stand against her.[4] At this time Rome was working to make herself mistress of the road leading to the country of the Volsci, and this thrust to the south was made at the cost of Ardea and the nearby Latin cities.[5] Although the treaty with Ardea known as the *foedus Ardeatinum*, brought pacification for a time, civil disorder amongst the inhabitants themselves, accompanied by war with the Volsci, caused further trouble.[6] Rome interfered only to celebrate a triumph over the Volsci, and to become mistress of Ardea.[7] The Romans were quick to make full use of the strategic importance of Ardea as a barrier against the Volsci, and as a safeguard to the ports on the Laurentian sea-board,[8] and in consequence another scene follows in her troubled history when she was made a Roman colony.[9]

During the Gallic wars of the beginning of the fourth century, Ardea was closely bound to Rome, and she was the scene of a few local successes. The city was honoured by Marcus Furius Camillus when he chose it as his place of exile.[10] The

[1] Dion. Hal., *A.R.*, V, 61, 3.
[2] H. Last, *C.A.H.*, VII, 488; Carcopino, *V.O.O.*, 1919, p. 228 sq.
[3] H. Last, *ibid.*, p. 491; Boëthius, *B.M.*, June-July 1931, p. 7.
[4] Cf. Livy, III, 72. This is clearly seen in the case when territory disputed between Ardea and Aricia was annexed by Rome who had been invited to arbitrate.
[5] Piganiol, *La Conquête Romaine*, 1927, p. 84.
[6] Livy, IV, 9.
[7] According to Diodorus, XII, 34, this took place in 434 B.C.
[8] Boëthius, *B.M.*, June-July 1931, p. 8.
[9] Livy, IV, 2. Boëthius, *ibid.*, accepting as correct Livy's statement that colonists were settled there for defence against the Volsci, concludes that the old town was revived by the Romans to serve them in the campaign against the Volsci, and especially to keep them away from the ports on the Laurentian coast. See also Diodorus, XII, 34 (434), and Rosenberg, *Hermes*, LIV (1919), p. 156. Ardea was one of the earliest of Roman colonies; the decree of the senate by which she was given a fairly independent status served as a model for colonial administration. See H. Last, *C.A.H.*, VII, 503, who considers that the record of her colonization should not be rejected.
[10] Servius, *Ad Aen.*, VI, 825; Livy, V, 43-55; Plut., *Camillus*, 23, 24.

tide of unrest again passed over Ardea in the fourth century
during the Latin wars. Though little is recorded of any part
which she herself played in the struggle, Livy mentions raids
by the men of Antium who overran the *ager Ardeas* as well as
that of Ostia and the *ager Solonius* in 339 or 340 B.C.[1] It
appears that her one-time prosperity continued steadily to
diminish, for in 209 B.C. she was one of the twelve colonies[2]
which could not afford to send help to Rome during the second
Punic war. After this time she ceases to have any appreciable
place in historical records.[3]

In the time of Hadrian an appeal was made for the re-
distribution of her land,[4] and in the middle ages[5] a *castellum
Ardeae* was known, the appearance of which can have been
little different from that of the present day. In the eleventh
century Ardea was purchased by the Cesarini, a noble Italian
family, and in 1564 she passed to the Colonnesi.[6] The ruin
and desolation of Ardea was perhaps not altogether due to the
fortunes of war. The district at some time became unhealthy
as a result of the development of malaria, and was notoriously
dangerous in Augustan and later times, as can be learnt from
Classical writers.[7]

The tradition of Ardea's great antiquity, of her early prosperity and later decline, is supported by archaeological finds.
The bronze objects found by Professor Lugli in the northern
part of the acropolis in the spot called La Croce, amongst them
four fibulae of an archaic type with wire-like bows, and small
wheels with projecting hubs, are characteristic of the first
period of the Iron Age, and are typically Villanovan.[8] Pigorini's[9] finds, which he unearthed as long ago as 1882, in the

[1] Livy, VIII, 12: *Antiates in agrum Ostiensem Ardeatem Solonium incursiones fecerunt.*
[2] Livy, XXVII, 9. In this passage the colonies are loosely termed Latin. There appears,
however, to be no doubt that Ardea was a *Roman* colony; see above, p. 36, note 9.
[3] In 86 B.C. one of the leaders of the Bacchanalian riots was sent to Ardea in chains:
Livy, XXXIX, 9.
[4] Hadrian, *Lib. Colon.*, p. 231.
[5] Nibby, *Analisi della Carta dei Dintorni di Roma*, vol. I, 1848[2], p. 231.
[6] Hare, *Walks Round Rome*, 1906, p. 250.
[7] Strabo, V, 232; Martial, IV, 60; Seneca, *Ep.*, 105; Servius, *Ad Aen.*, VII, 796.
[8] Boëthius, *B.M.*, June-July 1931, p. 2, and Plate II.
[9] Pigorini, *B.P.I.*, VIII, 1882, p. 114. The finds are stated to have been made in
the bank of the Incastro near the acropolis, whereas Boëthius, *loc. cit.*, says they came to
light in the *Campo Santo*. If Pigorini meant the side of the Incastro away from the
stream then there is no discrepancy. There are also short notes on these finds in Pasqui,
N.S., 1900, p. 54.

ground of the modern cemetery in the Civitavécchia, represented by a reticulate vase decorated on the outside with thick bands, like a net, a small fictile brazier with square base, and a group of six fibulae, three of the archaic bow-fibula type, and three of the fully-developed *navicella* or boat-shaped type[1] are also indicative of the same culture,[2] though the latter type of fibula goes down to a later date than the other finds. There can accordingly be no doubt that Ardea takes her place among the southern centres of the Latian Villanovan culture, and is contemporary with the settlements in Rome and the Alban hills where similar finds have been made.[3] Thus the tradition of her antiquity is archaeologically confirmed. Although the finds belonging to this age are yet sporadic, and the Iron Age (Villanovan) cemetery has not yet been located for a certainty, the early beginnings of the history of Ardea cannot be questioned, and it is clear that excavation has still much to yield.

In these Iron Age settlers the first comers to the rock of Ardea may be recognized, and Strabo's words are confirmed when he speaks of the Rutuli as inhabiting ancient Ardea:[4] 'Ρούτουλοι οἱ τὴν ἀρχαίαν 'Αρδέαν ἔχοντες.' Perhaps the greatest significance of these typical Villanovan objects is the light they throw on the racial origins of the Rutuli, for they are proved to have been of a Latin[5] stock analagous and contemporary with the earliest inhabitants of Rome and the Alban hills. The latest computation, that of Åberg,[6] would put the date of the first appearance of the Villanovan culture in Latium as not much earlier than 750 B.C. By a strange chance this is roughly contemporary with the traditional date of the founding of Rome which is variously given as 752 or 753 B.C.; thus archaeology does not confirm the tradition that Ardea was older than Rome, or that the city existed as an inhabited site in Trojan times, or at the time of the fall of Troy which is usually put at about 1220 to 1200 B.C.

---

[1] Illustrated Boëthius, *B.M.*, June-July 1931, Pl. II, 2 and 3.

[2] Bernabei, exploring in the same place, found more objects like those discovered by Pigorini, and also a cup and two lunate-handled vases.

[3] Boëthius, *B.M.*, June-July 1931, p. 2; cf. also R. MacIver, *Villanovans and Early Etruscans*, 1924, p. 70 sq., Åberg, *Bronzezeitliche und Früheisenzeitliche Chronologie*, Teil I, Italien, 1930, p. 216.

[4] Strabo, V, 228.

[5] Boëthius, *B.M.*, June-July 1931, p. 3.

[6] Åberg, *ibid.*, pp. 211, 212, and 217.

In a much later time chamber tombs[1] belonging to the fourth and third centuries, found by Pasqui outside Casalazarro along the old road leading towards Lanúvio, perhaps give some indication of the economic conditions of the inhabitants in that age: they were of one room only, and of poor construction; the furniture consisted mostly of coarse black glazed Campanian ware, sherds of red earthenware and a few minor objects in bronze. The general poverty of the tombs and their contents is significant; they belonged to the populace who lived under the Roman colonization and experienced the troublous times of the Latin wars. Nothing could better demonstrate Ardea's decline in these centuries than the poverty of the wayside tombs lining what had formerly been one of her most important lines of communication.[2]

The most impressive of the monuments of Ardea are her defence works. The acropolis stands about thirty metres above the surrounding valleys, with precipitous sides offering to an enemy a bare rock face and vertical ascent. At some epoch, most probably by the earliest settlers, it was cut off from the lower platform of Civitavécchia by means of an artificial trench on the east side, making an easily defensible area of rock plateau. In places where the rock of the acropolis was not sufficiently strong and steep, it was buttressed with a wall of local tufa, especially on the east where the fortifications were made particularly secure and the whole was faced with a wall. The ruins which now remain, together with the tower flanking the gateway, are a patchwork of mediaeval restorations.[3] On the north and west sides of the rock no traces are to be seen of ancient defence works, and it is noticeable that those on the east indicate the direction from which danger was to be feared at the time when they were made, facing, as they do, the country of the Volsci and Aricini and the extension of the city over the plateaux of Civitavécchia and Casalazarro. It is probable that in Roman times and in the early settlement there was no gate on the western side, and that the acropolis

---

[1] These are described in detail by Pasqui, *N.S.*, 1900, p. 56 sq.

[2] Other excavations in 1897 financed by the University Museum of Philadelphia revealed a variety of pottery, but add nothing to our present knowledge. See Louise Adams Holland, *B.M.*, October-January 1933-4, p. 5 sq., where a complete account is given. The vases are housed in the Pennsylvania Museum.

[3] The walls were surveyed by Professor Boëthius and members of the Swedish School at Rome: *B.M.*, June-July 1931 *passim*; and Pl. LII, 2.

presented an unbroken front to those approaching either from the direction of the sea or from Rome,[1] and that the gateway on the east, the entrance of which is probably *in situ*, was the only approach to the citadel proper.

The two roads, one connecting Ardea with Rome, and the other, the older way of communication, leading to the inland and hill cities of Latium, must have converged on this gate. The former, the ancient Via Ardeatina,[2] thus made a circuit of the rock on the south to enter by the ramp leading up to the eastern gate. This manner of approach is strategic, causing an enemy to expose his right side in making the turn; the same kind of entrance is to be found at Lavinium.[3] The modern road from Rome leads up to the western gate and two roads branch off from within the entrance and cross the top of the acropolis, passing through the present habitation. The level as it is seen now is not that of Roman times as is learned not only from the fact that these roads are deeply worn into the soft tufa, but also that they cut through ancient tunnels and underground granaries.[4]

It is on the east again that the most remarkable work of defence is found, significant of the need of protection from the cities farther inland and in the hills. Bounding Civitavécchia where the plateau, itself well fortified naturally by steep slopes on the north and south, becomes narrower, stands a high earth mound[5] with a deep and wide ditch before it. It strengthens what would otherwise have been a weak place in the city's defences (pl. 16). The ditch is crossed by an embankment faced once with masonry, along which runs the main road from Ardea to Lanúvio (ancient Lanuvium) and the hills. The remains of the gate[6] of the long corridor type are seen in a few

[1] Boëthius, *B.M.*, June-July 1931, p. 6. The present archway and tower are of eleventh-century workmanship, said to have been built by Cencio Savelli.

[2] Dr. Axel Boëthius informed the writer that the modern so-called Via Laurentina follows the ancient road for about the first ten, and the last six kilometres.

[3] See below, p. 55-6.

[4] Boëthius, *B.M.*, June-July 1931, p. 6, considers that the presence of the tunnels and granaries proves that the roads are not ancient. These were found by members of the Swedish School in Rome to run upwards towards the ridge of the acropolis from the sides. They were probably drains typical of Campagna cities. See also Richter, *A.I.*, 1884, p. 102 sq., whose theories have by now been for the most part superseded.

[5] Sestini, *B.M.*, August 1930, p. 8 sq.

[6] Probably of the same type as that of Lanuvium, with two square bastions, and of the Porta di Ercolano at Pompeii: Boëthius, *B.M.*, June-July 1931, p. 13.

blocks of stone left at each side of the road where it pierces the mound.[1]

One of the greatest archaeological problems concerning Ardea is the dating of the defences. The trench isolating the acropolis cannot for certain be assigned to any particular epoch. It may be as old as the first settlement, as perhaps is indicated by the position of the graves in Civitavécchia found by Pasqui,[2] but conversely may have originated in the later history of the city when the populace was probably confined to the area of the acropolis.

The walls are assigned by Boëthius[3] to the first century B.C., to the time of the civil wars, because the populace was, in his opinion, then reduced to a handful remaining on the acropolis; they thus belong to the time when Roman Italy was fortified anew to protect the power of the Senate. The more recent interpretation of Säflund on the other hand would date them to the time of the Gracchi and compare them with the group on the Aventine hill at Rome.[4] There is the possibility that the populace was reduced in number after the Samnite wars of the third century B.C. which would make the walls comparable with those of Falerii Novi which are known historically to be later than 241 B.C., the time of the Roman conquest of Falerii Veteres.

The earth mound and ditch are comparable with Roman work[5] of the fourth century and the Volscian defences of Antium: Säflund considers this work probably equal in date with the so-called Servian *agger*, though he would point out that an earth mound is a characteristic defence work in all western Europe from as early as neolithic times.[6] He considers that it constituted the whole fortification of Ardea until the fourth century, and suggests that it may go back to the Iron Age.[7] Boëthius puts it as not later than 400 B.C., since in his opinion after that time no defence facing in this direction or in this part of the city was needed.[8]

[1] The mound is so high that it is said that at sunset it can easily be seen from Albano by the shadow cast behind it. Hare, *Walks Round Rome*, 1906, p. 251.
[2] See above, p. 37, and note 9.
[3] Boëthius, *B.M.*, April-July 1934.
[4] Säflund, *Le Mura di Roma Repubblicana*, 1932, p. 253.
[5] Boëthius, *B.M.*, June-July 1931, p. 14.
[6] Säflund, *ibid.*, pp. 124, 231.
[7] Boëthius and Van Buren found that the soil underneath contained only sherds of the first periods of the Iron Age.
[8] Mr. C. A. Ralegh Radford has pointed out to the writer that it must be later than the graves in Civitavécchia, and earlier than those in Casalazarro as its position shows, because the graves would be situated outside the limits of the city.

It is therefore fairly safe to conclude that this earthwork, which is of almost majestic proportions, gave shelter against the men of the hills, the Volsci, who from earliest times until their domination by the Romans coveted the plains and access to the sea.

Such was the inherited tradition of Ardea in the Augustan age; she was known to Vergil and his circle as a city of reputed antiquity, with a once glorious past, but whose fortune had long since vanished. To the poet's thought she was a pattern of fame that perishes, and his own words speak of her plight:

> *locus Ardea quondam*
> *dictus avis et nunc magnum manet Ardea nomen*
> *sed fortuna fuit.*[1]

Strabo[2] gives a most valuable record of the ruinous state into which she had fallen in that age, when he speaks of her together with Lavinium as only 'traces of cities', 'ἴχνη πόλεων'; and his words are in full accord with Vergil's designation of the city as *locus*. Her destruction, according to Strabo, was due to the ravages of the Samnites, but doubt remains about which wars this statement reflects. Some authorities consider that they are the wars of the third century B.C., and it can be argued that the failure of Ardea to send help in the second Punic war is thus accounted for,[3] or it is possible that Ardea was devastated during the Marian and Sullan wars of the beginning of the first century B.C., when Marius was helped by Samnites. Appian[4] describes how Marius in 87 B.C. overran Latium, taking Antium, Aricia, Lanuvium and other cities: the close proximity of Ardea gives reason to believe that she did not escape his triumphant advance, lying as she did on the route of his approach to the Via Appia. It may then have been in this century that Ardea became completely ruined. As has already been seen,[5] by the time of the Augustan age, or even earlier, the whole district had become unhealthy owing to the spread of malaria, causing it to be deserted. We turn again to Strabo[6]

---

[1] *Aen.*, VII, 411-13, imitated by Sil. It., I, 293: *magnanimis regnata viris, nunc Ardea nomen.*

[2] Strabo, V, 232. His calculation that Ardea is at a distance of seventy stades from the sea is erroneous; the distance is not more than thirty.

[3] See above, p. 37, and Boëthius, *Roma*, XVII, p. 15.

[4] App., *Bell. Civ.*, I, 69 (313).

[5] See above, p. 37, and Introduction, pp. xii-xiii.

[6] Strabo, V, 231; also Martial, IV, 60; Sen., *Ep.*, 105, 1; Servius, *Ad Aen.*, VII, 796.

for a contemporary account; he says with reference to Latium:
'ἅπασα δ'ἐστὶν εὐδαίμων καὶ παμφόρος πλὴν ὀλίγων χωρίων τῶν κατὰ τὴν παραλίαν, ὅσα ἑλώδη καὶ νοσερά, οἷα τὰ τῶν Ἀρδεατῶν'. 'All is prosperous and productive except a few places near the coast which are marshy and unhealthy, such as the district of Ardea.'

In spite of her desolation, many picturesque legends were attached to her name, which were current in the Augustan age, and familiar to Vergil. According to the best-known tradition she received a Mycenaean foundation which was attributed to Danae, the daughter of Acrisius, the Argive king, and the mother of Perseus. This story is twice referred to in the *Aeneid*:

> audacis Rutuli ad muros, quam dicitur urbem
> Acrisioneis Danae fundasse colonis
> praecipiti delata Noto.[1]

also

> et Turno, si prima domus repetatur origo,
> Inachus Acrisiusque patres mediaeque Mycenae.[2]

Servius gives the picturesque story in greater detail. When Danae had been violated by Jupiter, her father Acrisius shut her in a chest, and consigned her to the sea. She was carried by the waves to the coast of Italy where a fisherman found her cast upon the shore; with her was her new-born child, Perseus.[3] She was taken to the king, Pilumnus, who made her his wife, and together with him she founded Ardea. So did Turnus,[4] prince of Ardea, trace his descent from Mycenaean kings.[5]

As has already been shown, there is no archaeological evidence to confirm the legend of a Mycenaean or even a Greek origin.[6] So far, no Mycenaean remains have been found along the west coast of Italy, although numerous finds have been made in Sicily. Catherine Saunders[7] suggests that a site such as that of Ardea, within view and easy reach from the sea, could hardly be left untouched by trade connections of early times.

---

[1] *Aen.*, VII, 409-11. [2] *Aen.*, VII, 371-2.
[3] Servius, *Ad Aen.*, VII, 371.
[4] Cf. Pliny, *N.H.*, III, 56, 5: *Ardea a Danae Persei matre condita*; and Solinus, 2, 5.
[5] A less common tradition attributed the city's foundation to Ardea, son of Ulysses and Circe: Xenagoras *apud* Dion. Hal., *A.R.*, 472; Stephanus of Byzantium, *sub voce* "Ἀρδέα'.
[6] See above, p. 38 sq. [7] *Vergil's Primitive Italy*, 1930, p. 33.

It may be that in the brisk trading activities of the eighth and seventh centuries, Greek tales came in with Greek wares. It is also worthy of remark that the Greeks were settled at Cumae at the end of the ninth century,[1] and from there may have extended their influence as far north as the coastal cities of Latium. In the absence of any Greek remains in the soil of Ardea, the story (tempting as it is with a suggestion of a Mycenaean origin) can only be regarded as one fabricated at a time when Greek legends were fashionable, perhaps as an offshoot of the traditionalizing tendency of the Augustan age, and not as a reflection or memory of pre-Classical times.

The name of Ardea was thought by some ancient writers to be descriptive of the steep-sided and towering acropolis: 'Ardea quasi ardua dicta est, id est magna et nobilis.'[2] Another suggestion comes from Hyginus, quoted by Servius, that the name is derived from augury, which, as practised among the Romans, was a religious system of obtaining omens from ritual observation of the flight of birds.[3] Others would refer it to the Latin name for a species of heron,[4] and another picturesque legend tells how Ardea gave her name to the bird. After the death of Turnus, so it runs, there flew up from the ashes of the burning city a bird, pale, emaciated, and weak in cry, typifying her destruction, and mourned for her with the beating of its wings. Thereafter the bird was called *ardea* after the city. This seems to be such a personification of a city as was popular in the age when Ovid wrote in the *Metamorphoses*:

> cadit Ardea, Turno
> *sospite dicta potens; quem postquam barbarus ensis*
> *abstulit et tepida latuerunt tecta favilla,*
> *congerie et media tum primum cognita praepes*
> *subvolat et cineres plausis everberat alis.*
> *et sonus et macies et pallor et omnia, captam*
> *quae deceant urbem.   nomen quoque mansit in illa*
> *urbis et ipsa suis deplangitur Ardea pennis.*[5]

In view of the condition of Ardea and her notorious un-

---

[1] Åberg, *Bronzezeitliche und Früheisenzeitliche Chronologie*, Teil I, Italien, 1930, p. 213.

[2] Servius, *Ad Aen.*, VII, 411.   [3] Servius, *ibid.*, 412.

[4] It is perhaps noteworthy that Vergil's words in *Aen.*, VII, 412, quoted on p. 42 above, *dictus avis* might be taken to mean 'called [by the name of] a bird'.

[5] Ovid, *Met.*, XIV, 573 sq.

healthiness, the question arises as to why in an age so glorious any interest should attach to her, ruined and remote as she was, and why she should be given prominence in the *Aeneid*, the crowning literary achievement of the time. The legends alone cannot have had such attraction for the poet whose desire was to exalt the Roman race. The ancient records, however, give evidence for the existence of several cults at, or in the neighbourhood of, Ardea, and Strabo's[1] notice again provides the key, for we owe to him the knowledge of a temple sacred to Venus near the city where the Latins held federal cults: the legend of Aeneas, he says, brought it fame, and the ceremonies observed there were said to have originated in his time.[2] The ancient sanctuaries on her soil lived on, and worship was continued. Around them the Aeneas-cycle of legend had increased, and perhaps at the federal gatherings the old tales were told, freshly informed from age to age, of the Trojan invasion, and the fall of the passionate prince of Ardea. It was without doubt the religious significance of the city as a cult-centre which claimed the poet's regard.

Historical as well as literary records go far to prove Strabo's statement, and to show Ardea's inherited position in the religious life of the Latins. In 217 B.C. Ardea was one of the centres where especially great sacrifices were offered as a measure to check the advance of Hannibal after Trebia.[3] An event of 199 B.C. shows the power the Rutuli retained of claiming their religious rights, although their economic greatness was now past, when they protested to the Senate because they had not received their due portion of sacrifice at the *Feriae Latinae*, the federal Latin festival held annually in honour of Jupiter Latiaris on the summit of the Alban hill where his temple stood. As a result of this protest the *Feriae* were repeated by a decree of the high priests (*pontifices*).[4]

---

[1] Strabo, V, 232: ἔστι δὲ καὶ ταύτης πλησίον 'Αφροδίσιον ὅπου πανηγυρίζουσι Λατῖνοι. Σαυνῖται δ'ἐπόρθησαν τοὺς τόπους καὶ λείπεται μὲν ἴχνη πόλεων, ἔνδοξα δὲ διὰ τὴν Αἰνείου γέγονεν ἐπιδημίαν καὶ τὰς ἱεροποιίας, [ἃς] ἐξ ἐκείνων τῶν χρόνων παραδεδόσθαι φασί.

[2] Malten, *Aineias, Archiv für Religionswissenschaft*, XXIX, 1931-2, has shown how the legend of Aeneas originated in the Troas where Anchises was connected with the worship of Aphrodite, and came to be regarded as the father of Aeneas: as a result, Aeneas was connected with places having a cult of Aphrodite (or Venus) and especially that of Aphrodite-Aineas. The question of the etymology of this epithet is discussed by Boas, *Aeneas' Arrival in Latium, Allard Pierson Stichting, Archaeologisch-Historische Bydragen*, VI, 1938, p. 9.

[3] Livy, XXII, 1, 19: *decemviri Ardeae in foro maioribus hostiis sacrificarunt.*

[4] Livy, XXXII, 1.

The existence of a cult and temple of Juno at Ardea is clearly attested both by Vergil himself and by Pliny.[1] In the *Aeneid* when the fury Allecto incites Turnus to wrath she appears to him in the guise of an old woman, the priestess of Juno; her cheeks become wrinkled, and she binds her hoary locks with a fillet entwining therein a wreath of olive:

> *in vultus sese transformat anilis*
> *et frontem obscenam rugis arat, induit albos*
> *cum vitta crinis, tum ramum innectit olivae;*
> *fit Calybe Iunonis anus templique sacerdos.*[2]

Thus transformed she reminds him that the sceptre of the Latins is denied him and that a stranger shall receive his own promised bride and kingdom, and urges him to avenge his wrongs, to make war on the Trojans, and even to demand satisfaction from Latinus himself. These behests, she says, are at the express command of the daughter of Saturn herself:

> *'ipsa palam fari omnipotens Saturnia iussit'.*[3]

In answer Turnus only scoffs at the pretended priestess:

> *'cura tibi divum effigies et templa tueri'.*[4]

But then the Fury works her evil will by revealing her true self to Turnus and inciting him to impulsive action.

Pliny writes as though he had actually seen this temple of Juno at Ardea, which is not an impossibility since, as he tells us, it was famous in his day for some paintings on its walls done by an Asiatic artist: 'decet non sileri et Ardeatis templi pictorem, praesertim civitate donatum ibi et carmine quod est in ipsa pictura his versibus:

> *dignis digna. loco picturis condecoravit*
> *reginae Iunonis supremi coniugis templum*
> *Plautius Marcus, cluet Asia lata esse oriundus*
> *quem nunc et post semper ob artem hanc Ardea laudat.*

eaque sunt scripta antiquis litteris Latinis'.[5] The language of the verses seems to indicate a date in the second century B.C.[6] This passage seems to suggest, too, that the temple was not

---

[1] *N.H.*, XXXV, 115.   [2] *Aen.*, VII, 416-19.   [3] *Aen.*, VII, 428.
[4] *Aen.*, VII, 443.   [5] Pliny, *N.H.*, XXXV, 115.
[6] Boëthius, *B.M.*, June-July 1931, p. 4.

abandoned in Pliny's time, and may even have been in a good state of preservation. Thus not only the cult, but the actual temple could have been known to Vergil.

Pliny[1] also mentions pictures older than Rome herself, which he admired beyond all others because they were preserved in their original freshness although the buildings were roofless. It is plain that these also were actually seen by Pliny in person because he compares them with others which remained at Lanuvium, nude figures of Atalanta and Helen, side by side, done by the same artist as those at Ardea, and uninjured although the temple was in ruins. These were so lifelike, he says, that the Emperor Caligula was fired with passion for them, and would have removed them had the stucco allowed. These paintings, preserved so remarkably at Ardea, in outline technique, reputed even in ancient days to be older than Rome, undoubtedly were similar to the Graeco-Etruscan work to be seen at Tarquinia and Veii. It is quite possible that by the word 'aedibus' Pliny may mean tombs, which perhaps to him looked like small ruined shrines. The use of the word is noticeable because it could not indicate an important building such as the temple of Juno which he would surely designate as 'templum'. The date of these paintings is probably to be assigned to the sixth or seventh centuries.

Some authorities would combine this passage with the one already quoted above concerning the Temple of Juno, considering that one and the same building is described. There is nothing to be found in favour of this supposition, as a close consideration of the text will prove. In one there are 'aedes sacrae', in the other a 'templum'; in one the painter is not mentioned by name, in the other it is Plautius Marcus. The paintings in the one are so old that they are estimated to be older than Rome, in the other the account is given just before the writer goes on to discuss mural painting in the age of Augustus. In the older manner the names are written beside the figures in the Etruscan style, in the later one there is a hexameter verse in old-fashioned lettering but in good Latin, a thing which could not appear in a painting reputed to be older than Rome. It is to be concluded that Pliny saw in Ardea

---

[1] *N.H.*, XXXV, 17. Boethius, *B.M.*, June-July 1931, p. 4, considers that these were similar to the archaic Graeco-Etruscan work to be seen at Tarquinia and Veii. See also Jex-Blake and Sellers, *The Elder Pliny's Chapters on the History of Art*, 1896, pp. 85-7.

ruined shrines or possibly tombs, painted in the Etruscan manner, and in addition a temple to Juno containing famous paintings by a well-known artist, the first belonging to possibly the seventh century, the other to the second or first b.c.

Servius[1] speaks of a temple sacred to Castor and Pollux which, he finds evidence to show, was probably known to Vergil. Commenting on the lines in the first book of the *Aeneid* in which is recounted Juno's outburst against the Trojans, her anger at her own failure to destroy them, and her recollection that Pallas once was given the power to set the Greek fleet on fire and even to slay Ajax, the son of Oileus, he relates how some saw in the description of his death a reference to the picture which could be seen in the temple behind the door on the left hand side. This showed Capaneus pierced through both his temples by a thunderbolt: 'nam Ardeae in templo Castoris et Pollucis in laeva intrantibus post forem Capaneus pictus est fulmen per utraque tempora traiectus.' In Vergil, Pallas hurls from the clouds the swift thunderbolt of Jupiter, strikes the fleet, and makes the sea tumultuous with the winds, piercing the victim of her wrath with the fires of lightning and impaling him on a jagged rock:

> *ipsa Iovis rapidum iaculata e nubibus ignem,*
> *disiecitque rates evertitque aequora ventis,*
> *illum exspirantem transfixo pectore flammas*
> *turbine corripuit scopuloque infixit acuto.*[2]

Archaeological evidence goes far to confirm the documentary statements of Ardea's importance as a religious centre where ancient cults continued to be observed. Beyond Strabo's[3] statement, very little is known concerning the temple of Venus. It is mentioned in the elder Pliny's list of places lying on the Latian sea-board,[4] but his list gives no topographical evidence: 'in principio est Ostia ... oppidum Laurentum, lucus Iovis Indigetis, amnis Numicius, Ardea, Aphrodisium, Antium'.[5] Our present knowledge will not permit any certain location of the Temple of Venus, Pliny's Aphrodisium, but the importance of such a cult, and its fame, cannot be overlooked. The

---

[1] Servius, *Ad Aen.*, I, 44.   [2] *Aen.*, I, 42-5.   [3] See above, p. 45.

[4] Pliny, *N.H.*, III, 56; cf. Mela, *Itin.*, II, 4: *Ostia, Laurentum, Ardea, Aphrodisium, Antium.*

[5] Although the wording might seem to suggest a location south of Ardea, yet it may just as reasonably mean that the temple site was at Ardea.

PLATE 24. The Fosso dell' Incastro (see page 69)

PLATE 25. The Rio Torto at Santa Procula (see page 69)

sites, however, of two temples have been found but not as yet
identified, and in recent years an early basilica has been excavated which is thought to have some connection with the Latin
federal gatherings mentioned by Strabo.[1]

Of the two temples that have been discovered at Ardea, one
was on the acropolis and the other in Civitavécchia. The
remains of the former are to be seen under some modern
houses a little way past the fork in the road after the city has
been entered through the western gate. Tufa foundations and
remains of the stylobate can be distinguished and standing on
it, and partly incorporated in one of the houses is a considerable
fragment of a wall roughly faced with uneven stones (*opus
incertum*). This foundation was investigated in 1930 by the
Associazione Internazionale degli Studi Mediterranei.[2] It was
ascertained that the foundations were built of rows of headers
and stretchers, resting on the living rock: the blocks were sunk
into a great pit in the tufa stratum of the acropolis. Remains of
two heavy pilasters were also found. The wall of *opus incertum*
was perhaps the sustaining wall surrounding the area which
ran fairly close to the sides and rear wall of the temple.

Decorative terracotta ornaments and revetments in large
quantities came to light. The significant fact which emerges
from a study and classification of these fragments[3] is that they
belong to different epochs, and go to prove that the temple was
rebuilt or repaired at least three times.[4] They range from the
sixth to the first century B.C., thus tending to confirm the
supposed dating of Ardea's early prosperity, at the same time
pointing to continued and uninterrupted worship at these
temples, even when the city had ceased to be, and finally coming down to the age of Vergil himself.

Before these excavations in 1930 various other terracottas
came fortuitously to light at different times.[5] The feet of a
statue which must have been a little over life-size, have long
been known and are in the same museum as the fragments

---

[1] Strabo, V, 232.

[2] *B.M.*, Aug. 1930, Pl. II; June-July 1931, p. 5. Boëthius compares the foundation
works with those of the Capitol, and the enclosure wall with that of Juno Sospita at
Lanuvium.

[3] The fragments are housed in the Museo Villa Giulia in Rome.

[4] Andrèn, *B.M.*, June-July 1931, p. 17 sq. and drawings.

[5] Van Buren, *Figurative Terracotta Revetments in Etruria and Latium*, 1921, p. 20,
records an antefix from Ardea of fine workmanship; see *Cat. Mus. Campana*, IV, p. 25,
no. 27.

E

discussed above. They are painted red, and therefore belonged to a male figure, and are very carefully and faithfully modelled. They are supposed, by authorities, to be work of the fifth or fourth century B.C. There are also in the same case in the museum two revetments of yellowish clay probably of the third or fourth century. These are all thought to have come from the temple on the acropolis but throw no light on the problems connected with it, except for corroborating the tradition of prosperity in these early centuries. The identification of the acropolis temple remains uncertain. Its position in the centre of the most ancient and strategic quarter of the city points to a cult of no small local importance, perhaps even indicates that it was in origin the seat of the primitive worship of the first settlers on the rocky plateau. From the literary records we have to choose between the temple of Castor and Pollux and the temple of Juno, but further than that we cannot go, for it is not to be assumed that we have in literature the names of all the deities worshipped at Ardea.

The second temple was excavated in the lower part of the ancient city near the spot called Casa Linaccio (see plan, fig. 5) by Stefani in 1926,[1] and revealed little more than the platform (*podium*) of a shrine of small size with no indication of the deity to which it was dedicated (pl. 17). Vast quantities of decorative terracottas were found, however, which have been classified by Andrèn,[2] into four groups which range in date from the sixth to the first century B.C., and, as in the case of the acropolis temple, indicate an unbroken continuity of occupation and worship extending to the age of Vergil himself.

Excavations carried out in 1933 and 1934 by the Director and Students of the Swedish School at Rome revealed finds of major importance not only in the history of Ardea but in that of Roman architecture itself. The ground to the west of the temple was investigated, and the remains of a rectangular building were unearthed which has been reconstructed as a basilica of the first century B.C.[3] (fig. 7). The internal measurements of this building are 45.80 ms. long and 23.80 ms. wide, and the ancient walls are preserved in places to a height of 1.5 ms. They are constructed of a rubble core with a facing of lozenge-shaped stones (*opus reticulatum*).[4] The

---

[1] Wickèn, *B.M.*, April-July 1934, p. 7.   [2] Wickèn, *B.M.*, April-July 1934, p. 7.
[3] A full account is given *ibid.*, p. 7 sq.   [4] This shows quite clearly in pl. 18.

northern wall was pierced by three gates, and there was adjacent to it a water cistern. The middle gate led by a series of
four steps on to an open area at a slightly higher level than the
basilica proper. Against the eastern wall was found to abut a
portico higher than the floor of the basilica. Remains of seven
columns were evident. A gate in the eastern wall at its southern
end gave direct access from the basilica to the portico and the
portico also had communication with the temple, as is clearly
seen in the ramp, later cut into five steps, made out of the solid
rock, which gives access to the platform (pl. 18).

Along the southern side of the basilica were found traces of
two steps running along the whole length, and square bases
of pilasters, proving that the building was roofed. Sufficient
traces of fluted columns faced with stucco and standing on
bases of an Attic-Ionic type were left to allow a reconstruction
of two rows of nine columns parallel with the northern and
southern walls, and of four parallel with the short walls (see
plan, fig. 7). Herein are to be recognized all the characteristics of an early Roman basilica; and the nature of the building
materials all point to a date not later than the first century B.C.[1]
The full import of this date must not be overlooked, for it gives
yet another proof of the historical tradition of the city's life:
that she lived on, after her economic decline, in the memory
and holiness of her ancient sanctuaries. The very fact of
building activity in this century shows the full vitality of the
religious life long after the city's decline.

Perhaps it is permitted to recognize in this basilica of so
early a type, so closely connected with the adjacent temple,
with open area adjoining, and water-supply at hand, the
meeting-place of the Latins and the scene of their federal feasts.
Its shelter would be welcome to pilgrims coming from a distance, since the buildings of the once prosperous city were
reduced to ruins. Did they here exchange their money, barter
goods, and hold the revelry of a county fair before the worn
steps? Was it here on the feast days that the stories of Aeneas
were told and retold and handed on from generation to generation? Imagination can well clothe these poor ruins with scenes

---

[1] The basilica of Ardea takes its place among the very few early ones known to us,
and thus is of extreme importance in the history of the evolution of this kind of building.
It is thought to be contemporary with the early basilica at Pompeii, and to have had,
like it, a superstructure of wood.

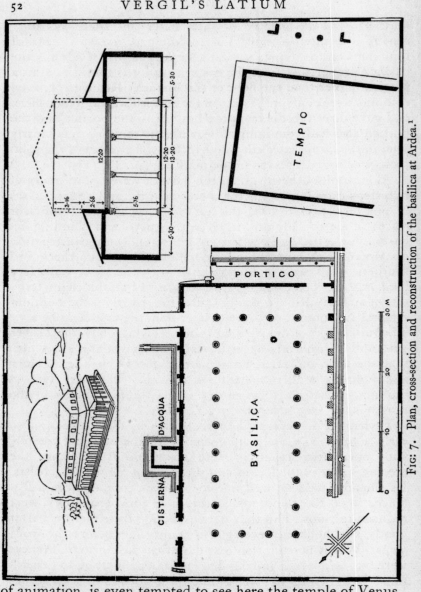

FIG. 7. Plan, cross-section and reconstruction of the basilica at Ardea.[1]

of animation, is even tempted to see here the temple of Venus, the Aphrodisium of Strabo's and of Pliny's notices.[2] Of this question no convincing answer can be given, but yet none may

[1] After Wickèn and Lindros, B.M., April-July 1934, pls. II, III.
[2] Strabo, V, 232; Pliny, N.H., III, 5.

deny that the poet may have seen here these federal gatherings
of which Strabo speaks, witnessed their rites and sacrifices,
and listened to the tales told at their sanctuaries.

It can hardly be doubted that Vergil at some time visited
Ardea. Access from Rome, along the Via Ardeatina, would
be easy, although the Campagna at that time was practically deserted, for the road must have been kept in repair for
the sake of the Roman magistrates whose duty it was to attend
the local festivals. Cicero[1] speaks of making a circuit of the
temples in the Ardeatine territory: 'cum fana circuimus in agro
Ardeati', perhaps in an official capacity, and it is even reasonable to recognize here a reference to the Latin cults mentioned
by Strabo. Doubtless *curiosi* and men of letters knew well her
ancient shrines which still existed on her soil in their day, and
perhaps went down from Rome to see them, drawn as much by
antiquarian, as by patriotic feeling.[2]

In making this supposition, a scene lies before us of Ardea
in the Augustan age as Vergil might have seen her. First
comes into view the acropolis dominating the landscape with
crumbling walls on the east and south. As the eastern gate is
entered there stands high the acropolis temple; the small
populace which perhaps remains to have charge of the sanctuaries, probably have their dwellings clustered round it.
From the summit of the rock are seen in the lower city amongst
the ruins of the older habitation, temples still standing, one of
them perhaps sacred to Venus, the divine mother of Aeneas,
and adjoining it the basilica for the housing of pilgrims. In
them are to be seen the famous paintings well known and
prized long after the Augustan age. Rounding off the city,
once a measure of defence, but now without function, rises the
majestic earth mound; beyond again are the ranges of the
Alban hills dominated by the Alban Mount. Such as this is
the Ardea which might have lain before the poet's gaze, a
place calculated to inspire his thought as he looked upon the
memorials of her vanished fortune, and on those ancient shrines[3]
so closely linked with the legendary history of his own people.

[1] Cicero, *D.N.D.*, III, 47.
[2] Varro, *R.R.*, II, 10, was familiar with her antiquities for he records an inscription
at Ardea which told how sheep-shearers first came into Italy from Sicily, 453 years
after the founding of Rome, led by Publius Titinius Maena.
[3] The cult of Juturna, also closely connected with Ardea, is discussed in the chapter
on the Numicus, p. 76 sq. below.

CHAPTER III

LAVINIUM

mihi moenia Teucri
constituent urbique dabit Lavinia nomen.[1]

PRATICA DI MARE, the modern habitation situated on the acropolis of ancient Lavinium,[2] lies at a distance of seventeen miles from Rome, and three miles from the shore. It can be reached by two different roads from Rome. If that, called at the present day, the Via Laurentina,[3] be followed, the branch at the cross-roads at Solforata which leads seawards, must be taken. This passes Castel di Leva and open fields of the Campagna. The road turns sharply to the right on approaching the city, and leads directly up to the gateway of the modern village, passing through an arch incorporated in the wall of the Palazzo (pls. 19 and 20), which has been in sight for several miles, conspicuous with its tower dominating the surrounding landscape.

Pratica may also be reached from Rome by the Via di Decima, which in part corresponds to the ancient Laurentina.[4] This branches off the Via Ostiensis, and passes by Malpasso, Decima, where a Roman milestone *in situ* marks the eleventh mile from Rome, and by Capocotta. This road has a truly Vergilian setting where it passes for a distance of several miles along the edge of the Laurentian forest in the glades of which the wild boar and stag can sometimes be seen.[5]

On approaching Pratica, this road slopes steeply upwards to the citadel, and then takes a sharp bend to the left to pass through the same gateway, the only entrance to the citadel proper and the habitation of to-day (pl. 20). The modern

---

[1] *Aen.*, XII, 193-4.

[2] The site has been identified beyond doubt from several inscriptions of the Imperial age bearing the name *Laurentes Lavinates*: see especially *C.I.L.*, XIV, 2069 (Dessau, *ibid.*, p. 186), 2070 sq.

[3] Now wrongly named, for it follows in part the ancient Ardeatina, and goes to Ardea.

[4] For details of the route of the ancient Via Laurentina, see below, p. 90 sq.

[5] See page xii in the Introduction.

village extends in the form of a square over part of the area of
what was once the ancient acropolis, and is walled in with
houses on all sides, built round a piazza in the middle of which
stands the church. The whole is overshadowed by the Palazzo,
a country seat of the Borghese family dating to the sixteenth
century. The village is in a poor condition, though not quite
as poverty-stricken as Ardea; the streets are not paved, and are
usually thickly strewn with straw. This place, like many others
on the Campagna, has been malaria-ridden, but the health
services and clinics of the Fascist government have done much
for the relief of the inhabitants, and the members of the
Borghese family take a philanthropic interest in the people.
Workers on the Campagna fields, for the most part, live at
Pratica, and in the evening it is a pleasant sight to see the herds
of white oxen being driven home through the arched gateway,
and to observe this obscure and forgotten life on the plains
which produces sturdy children, and kindly men and women.

The acropolis is about a mile in circuit, and stands about
eighty metres above the valley and lower-lying land. The
sides are precipitous in every part, not rocky like those of
Ardea, but grass grown. The northern part of the acropolis,
now uninhabited and merely a grassy plateau projecting beyond the village, stands a little higher than the rest. It is
possible to walk through the piazza and to come out onto its
grassy eminence. If a circuit be made at the foot of the
acropolis, starting from the eastern side, in a northward direction, it will be seen that a deep and wide trench isolates it on
this side. This may have been worked artificially, for there is
no appearance of its having been a water-course at any time;
the citadel from this point gives an impression of dominance
and majesty as can be seen in pl. 19. The trench runs into the
steep-sided valley of the Fosso di Pratica which half encircles
the citadel on the north, after rising only at a small distance
away on the east (pl. 23). The stream then reaches the modern
Via di Decima (the ancient Laurentina) where it is joined by the
small Rivo di Petronella; the combined waters pass under a
rustic bridge to join the sea three miles away. The road from
Rome skirts the foot of the acropolis on the western side, and
slopes steeply up to the arched gateway of the Palazzo, describing a sharp curve just before leading into the modern
village. There is every reason to suppose that the present

entrance is on the site of the ancient one, though no remains are visible; it is designed for tactical purposes, having a steep ramp, and by means of a bend turning to the left causing a man to expose his right side on approaching the city; and secondly no trace of a ramp can be seen at any other point, and the citadel appears always to have been completely isolated at all other points.

If this supposition be correct, then the citadel of Lavinium in this and several other respects is comparable with that of

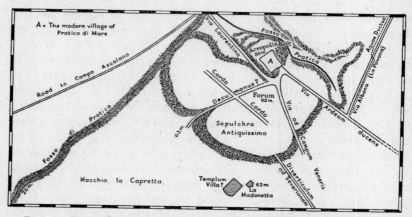

FIG. 8. Plan[1] of Lavinium, showing the acropolis, the extension of the city southwards and westwards and the various roads leading from it.

Ardea. Not only are both roughly elliptical in shape, but also each has a single entrance, planned for defence. Lavinium stands on the same outcrop of volcanic tufa, the last westward ridge of the Alban *massif*, as does Ardea. Fortification walls, however, like those at Ardea, are not now to be seen, although Nibby saw traces of old walls in the first half of the nineteenth century, which from his description appear to have been comparable with those still to be seen at Ardea to-day.[2] The tongue

---

[1] After Lanciani, *M.A.*, 1903.

[2] Nibby, *Analisi della Carta dei Dintorni di Roma*, vol. II, 1849[2], 234, speaks of having seen traces of old walls on the edge of the acropolis and in the 'artificial cutting in the rock on the north-east'; he describes them as *parallelipedi* of local rock that seem to be *in situ*, and mentions others in a ruinous state on the north-west side. The writer failed to find any remains of defence works in making a circuit of the acropolis; see also Lanciani, *M.A.*, 1903, p. 164.

of land giving immediate access to the gate appears to have
been narrowed artificially on both sides; a feature to be seen in
the Piazza d'Armi at Veii, at Gabii, and probably at Ardea, if
the trench isolating the eastern side of the acropolis was
artificially worked.

Just as the population of Ardea spread over the lower
plateau, so the same extension took place at Lavinium: the city
in this case stretched to the south and westward. The confines
are not in any sense defensive, for the edges of the plateau
slope gently to merge into the lower land. The acropolis must
have been the only possible place of defence, and topography
seems to indicate that the inhabitants of ancient Lavinium had
less to fear from their neighbours than had the people of Ardea.

Several roads lead out from Lavinium marking the site as
well centred, and suggesting her ancient designation as the
metropolis of the Latins;[1] see the plan (fig. 8). The oldest
line of communication was, as in the case of Ardea, east and
west, to the hills and to the sea. The road leading down from
Albano by way of La Pavona and Zolforata[2] lies probably on
this very ancient route. Another road leads to Ardea, a pleasant
way over the fields with a wide view of the sea and the mediaeval towers on the shore on the one hand, and on the other the
Alban ranges. It is impossible, however, to decide for a certainty whether this is ancient or not. The road leading to
Campus Veneris (see the plan, fig. 8) is certainly on the line of
a Roman road as one or two characteristic paving-stones of
black basalt can still be seen in place at a higher level than the
present surface. The unnamed road in the plan was probably the main street (*decumanus*), and the *cardo*, the branch
road, can be traced crossing over it. Its way now is through
tilled fields, but that the passer-by is in the midst of the old
city is known from the number of sherds and broken bricks
that strew the path, thrown up by the plough and thickly
scattered. This leaves the city and continues down to the sea.
Its course is quite straight, the surface sandy, and on each side
grow the trees of the forest, picturesque umbrella pines for the
most part. Such a road bears all the marks of Roman construction; the surface is crowned, and there is an edge of stone on
each side. This perhaps was the old road to the shore, and

[1] Dion. Hal., *A.R.*, V, 12.
[2] Ashby, *The Roman Campagna in Classical Times*, 1927, p. 209.

along it still pass the fishermen barefooted; and by the edge of it are some ruins of late Roman construction (pl. 21). Lastly, communication with Rome was afforded by means of the ancient Via Laurentina,[1] now followed in part by the modern Via di Decima.

The area over which extended the ancient city, now covered with vineyards and grassland, slopes gently down and merges into pasture and cultivated fields. These are bounded on the south and west by a belt of maritime forest, part of the Silva Laurentina which in Vergil's day covered all the Latian sea-board.[2] Thus then is the site of Lavinium, with an acropolis well defended by nature, connected with the surrounding country and neighbouring settlements by a good system of roads, three miles only from the sea, and holding a command-ing position on the ridge of tufa above the low-lying marsh-land and the sea-shore.

The ancient historians are rich in picturesque legends re-garding Lavinium, derived from sources which must have been equally accessible to Vergil. Their records tell of memorials to be seen there in his day of her legendary past, and of fanciful stories which grew up around them. Dionysius of Halicar-nassus[3] states that all historians agreed over the tradition that the city was founded by a band of Trojans led by Aeneas, escaped from the sack of Troy, and here ending their long wanderings. He tells of a straw hut kept sacred at Lavinium[4] which the inhabitants believed marked the spot where Aeneas sacrificed the white sow of prophecy and her thirty young, and which no stranger was allowed to enter because of its sanctity. He further suggests that the hut was thought to have been the place where Aeneas built his temple to the *Penates* whose wor-ship he established at Lavinium. This hut sanctuary was probably similar both to that of Romulus[5] preserved on the Palatine, and to the other hut on the Capitol; both of these are known to have been round with a thatched roof, and always to have been restored after a fire in the old-fashioned form. They may well have come down from the time of reed hut settle-ments and their primitive cults, in which even a sacred building

---

[1] For details, see below, p. 90 sq.
[2] See the Introduction, p. xii.
[3] Dion. Hal., *A.R.*, I, 55, sq.; cf. Aur. Vict., *De Or. G.R.*, 12.
[4] Vergil locates the prodigy on the banks of the Tiber, *Aen.*, VIII, 81-5.
[5] Platner and Ashby, *Topographical Dictionary of Rome*, 1929, *sub voce* 'Casa Romuli.'

must have been constructed of thatch: their modern counterparts are to be seen in the shepherds' straw huts (*capanne*) described in the Introduction.[1] Religious conservatism which lingers long and dies hard preserved their place and type.[2]

We learn from Varro[3] that bronze images of the sow and her thirty young were kept in a public place in Lavinium, in all probability the forum, and what was said to be the mother's body was preserved in salt and shown by the priests. He speaks of the tradition as being very ancient, and as if he himself saw the bronze statues: 'in quo illud antiquissimum fuisse scribitur quod sus Aeneae Lavini triginta porcos peperit albos . . . huius suis ac porcorum etiam nunc vestigia apparent, quod et simulacra eorum ahenea etiam nunc in publico posita, et corpus matris ab sacerdotibus quod in salsura fuerit, demonstratur.'

Dionysius[4] records a picturesque legend fabricated around other bronzes kept in the forum representing a wolf, a vixen, and an eagle. While the building of the city was in process there happened a prodigy. A fire broke out spontaneously in a neighbouring wood, and a wolf appeared trying to increase the conflagration, carrying in its mouth a piece of dry wood which it cast on the flames. At the same time an eagle came and fanned it with its wings. A vixen, however, dipped her tail into the river near by and tried thus to extinguish it. The other two then fell upon her, and in the end gained the mastery. Aeneas, witnessing this, took it as a good omen for his city. The historian saw the statues of these creatures in the forum, and remarks that they had been preserved there for a long time. Animal bronzes of this kind may indicate a local craft of early times, just as the sacred hut recalls the primitive settlement.

According to Dionysius, Lavinium was reputed to have been originally of very small extent, since, when Aeneas finally made peace with Latinus, he received the acropolis hill and land for a distance of forty stades around it;[5] two years after the founding, he goes on to state, the city became the metropolis of the Latin race, and so all Romans came to regard her.

[1] Introduction, p. xiii sq.
[2] It is well known that the Temple of Vesta in the Roman Forum, in its small round shape, derives from a primitive hut.
[3] Varro, *R.R.*, 11, 4.
[4] Dion. Hal., *A.R.*, I, 59.
[5] Dion. Hal., *A.R.*, I, 59; cf. Servius, *Ad Aen.*, XI, 316.

Thirty years after the foundation the seat of government was transferred to Alba Longa.[1] The *Penates*, however, were left behind at Lavinium, which henceforth became also the religious metropolis of the Latins, and so continued under the Romans.

The records of the city in semi-historical and historical times are scanty. Only one remarkable event is recorded in the time of the kings, the murder of Titus Tatius[2] when in the act of sacrificing to the *Penates*. The story may perhaps be regarded as preserving some memory of folk-lore, perhaps a primitive practice of the slaying of a king, or of a substitute for a king, and a subsequent trial for blood-guiltiness. The suggestion, however, that it was the duty of the king of Rome to carry out a priestly office in connection with the worship of the Lavinate *Penates* is full of significance. Tarquinius Collatinus[3] on resigning from the consulship retired to Lavinium to live in exile. This tradition is interesting in that it points to a hint of Etruscan influence in the late sixth century.

The Latin character of the inhabitants of Lavinium is clearly attested by the leading part they played in the Latin leagues of the sixth and fifth centuries which united to oppose the growing power of Rome. One of the two dictators of the league of the Thirty Cities which had its meeting-place at the *caput* (*aquae*) *Ferentinae* and with which Rome concluded the *foedus cassianum* early in the fifth century, was a man of Lavinium, Spurius Vecilius.[4] During the Gallic wars of the fourth century and the consequent revolt of many of the Latin cities, Lavinium seems to have stood firm for Rome together with Ardea and all the southern towns. Her loyalty was maintained during the Volscian invasion of the Campagna in the first half of the fifth century, and suffered siege by that half-legendary figure afterwards called Coriolanus.[5] Beyond an incident in the year 338 B.C. during the first Samnite war, when it was said that the citizens were at last induced to relax their

[1] Dion. Hal., *A.R.*, I. 63.

[2] Dion. Hal., *A.R.*, II, 52, 3; 53, 1; Livy, I, 14; Plutarch, *Romulus*, XXIII; Varro, *L.L.*, V, 152; Zonaras, VI, 4.

[3] Livy, II, 2; Dion. Hal., *A.R.*, V, 12.

[4] Dion. Hal., *A.R.*, III, 34, 3; Festus, p. 276. Later the name of the men of Lavinium appears in the list of the members of the Latin League which united to reinstate the kings. The list as given by Dionysius has, however, been questioned on good grounds; H. Last, *C.A.H.*, VII, p. 488; Carcopino, *V.O.O.*, 1919, p. 228 sq.

[5] Dion. Hal., *A.R.*, VIII, 21.

support of Rome, history is silent about Lavinium from that time onwards.[1] She goes down in oblivion until she re-emerges in different form in the time of Hadrian. By that time her name has changed, and some of the romance of her antiquity is gone. She comes under the imperial administration of the colonies, her forum is filled with statues dedicated with gratitude to emperors who renewed her institutions and she becomes the much be-ribboned cradle of the Roman race. Under the empire we know her henceforth as Laurolavinium.[2]

Though no systematic excavation has yet been conducted at Pratica di Mare, certain sporadic and chance discoveries have been made which, though scanty, give evidence of the habitation of this ancient site from earliest times down to the last Imperial ages. The various antiquities which have been unearthed at different times are all housed in the Palazzo Borghese on the site of the ancient city. They have been classified by Lanciani[3] into three periods, which he styles as 'archaic', 'middle', and 'Imperial', the first two of which are apposite to our inquiry. The finds belonging to the first period were unearthed in a spot near the edge of the south-western extension of the city, not far from where the forum is thought to have been. Judging from the nature of the objects it yielded, Lanciani reasonably supposed this place to have been the site of the earliest cemetery. In addition to other minor objects of bronze and iron, comprising rings, fibulae and bracelets, the low bowls of black glaze with reticulate pattern and small fictile braziers, and vases with *ansa bifora*, high handles pierced with two holes, are characteristic of the south Villanovan culture already established for Ardea.[4] The first inhabitants of Lavinium are thus seen to have belonged to that Latin stock which early reached Rome and the Alban hills,[5] and the site to

---

[1] Livy, VIII, 2. It is probable that Lavinium had her share in the general settlement of the Latin cities after the battle of Astura, and that the treaty was renewed between the citizens and Rome, and ordered to be renewed annually after the *Feriae Latinae*. Livy's designation *Laurentes* leaves some doubt as to whether he refers to the people of Lavinium.

[2] The new name appears first in Frontinus, *De Coloniis*, ap. Lachmann et Rudorff, *Feldmesser*, I, p. 234. Many of the inscriptions found on the site, all of imperial date, contain the double name *Laurentes Lavinates*. *C.I.L.*, XIV, 2069 sq. Most of them are to be seen in the Palazzo Borghese at Pratica.

[3] Lanciani, *M.A.*, 1903, p. 164 sq.

[4] See above, p. 38 sq.

[5] A fuller account of the finds from Lavinium is given in Catherine Saunders, *Vergil's Primitive Italy*, 1930, p. 61, taken from Helbig, *B.I.*, 1885, pp. 82-5.

be one of the primitive cities of the first-comers to the coastland of Latium.

An iron sword with T-shaped hilt[1] has misled some scholars into imagining that its presence at Lavinium gave proof of the tradition of the founding by a sea-farer of the late Mycenaean age.[2] The type is considered to be Mycenaean or sub-Mycenaean in origin and is widely diffused over central Italy. Specimens, mostly of iron, have been found at Corneto, Vetulonia, Terni, Veii, Rome, Conca (Satricum), Norcia, Capua, Cumae, and elsewhere. This type, however, cannot be of the very early date proposed, and the prototypes must have been many times imitated. It may have reached Lavinium overland from neighbouring cities, and no safe conclusion can therefore be made regarding its significance for overseas trade; we may not go so far as to say that herein is proof to be found of the Aeneas tradition, or even of early trade with the Mycenaean world.[3]

The finds of Lanciani's 'middle' period cover the last three centuries B.C. Terracotta revetments together with votive offerings in the form of a foot, an eye, and an ear, go down to the first century B.C.[4] and indicate probably a temple site. No identification, however, has so far been possible. The part of the city called Vignaccia was thought by Lanciani to have been the site of the forum because so many Doric tufa columns of an archaic form were discovered, but the finding of an archaic altar perhaps suggests rather the existence of a temple in this place with an altar before it. To Imperial times belong the many inscriptions which prove that here was the site of ancient Lavinium,[5] ranging from the time of Trajan down to the fourth century A.D. They indicate that the political existence of the city, and her ancient religious institutions lived again under the empire, and endured until its end.

For the Augustan age we have no records of history, but Strabo gives evidence of the condition of Lavinium as he did for Ardea; she lay in ruins brought to desolation by Samnite

---

[1] Illustrated, Lanciani, *M.A.*, 1903.

[2] Catherine Saunders, *Vergil's Primitive Italy*, 1930, p. 61. For a study of this type, see Randall McIver, *The Iron Age in Italy*, 1927, p. 183 and pl. 39.

[3] Catherine Sanders, *ibid*. She considers that the presence of Greek material with the sword confirms a settlement from overseas: in view of the possibility of overland routes from nearby cities, her supposition cannot be accepted unreservedly.

[4] All these can be seen in the Palazzo Borghese at Pratica di Mare.

[5] *C.I.L.*, XIV, 2069 sq. etc.

ravages,[1] and whether these belong to the Samnite wars of the
third century or of the civil war of Marius and Sulla in the
first century B.C., the tale is the same for Vergil's day. From
the close of the third century Lavinium sinks into insignificance and political oblivion. As is true of Ardea, however,
her sacred places and cults lived on, taking on fresh life
through the legendary connection with Aeneas, when the
Trojan cycle became popularized. Her name was not lost
because she remained one of the religious centres of Latium
where the old rites continued to be observed. She was the
home of the *Penates*[2] in Italy; on her citadel, the tradition went,
they were first settled, and given an abiding home by Aeneas
who had brought them safely from Troy through many dangers
by land and sea. This mission of his is one of the chief themes
of the *Aeneid* in its religious aspect:

> *sacra suosque tibi commendat Troia penatis;*
> *hos cape fatorum comites, his moenia quaere*
> *magna, pererrato statues quae denique ponto.*[3]

To political circles of the time the worship of the *Penates* at
Lavinium was a familiar duty which the magistrates of Rome
were bound by religious ties fully to observe.[4] Legend said
that although thirty years after the founding of Lavinium,
Ascanius transferred the government to Alba Longa, the
Penates were left behind in their original home.[5]

From the account of the murder of Titus Tatius of Lavinium,[6] it may perhaps be inferred that originally it was the duty
of the kings of Rome to make yearly sacrifices to the *Penates*,
and that later this sacred office passed to the consuls. From
Servius[7] and Macrobius[8] we learn that not only the consuls

[1] Strabo, V, 232; see above, p. 42.
[2] Vesta is joined with them in the *Aeneid*, though whether the designation *Penates*
includes her as well was not known even to the ancients; Servius, *Ad Aen.*, II, 296;
Macr., *Sat.*, III, 4, 11.
[3] *Aen.*, II, 293-5; cf. III, 12; 147-71, etc.
[4] The earliest literary reference is that of Varro, *L.L.*, III: *opidum quod primum
conditum in Latio, stirpis Romanae, Lavinium: nam ibi dii Penates nostri.* A Pompeian
inscription of the age of Claudius, dedicated to Sp. Turranius, gives further valuable
evidence: *C.I.L.*, X, 797: *sacra principia populi Romani Quiritium . . . apud Laurentes
coluntur.* See also Plut., *Coriol.*, 29; Dion. Hal., *A.R.*, I, 67.
[5] Dion. Hal., *A.R.*, LXIII. The myth is clearly aetiological.
[6] Plut., *Rom.*, 23.
[7] Servius, *Ad Aen.*, II, 296.
[8] Macr., *Sat.*, III, 4, 11.

but even the dictator, and the praetors and generals about to depart to their provinces[1] sacrificed at Lavinium, both on taking up and relinquishing office. In the time of Cicero,[2] Scaurus was proscribed because he had not taken care to see that the rites at Lavinium were properly carried out. C. Hostilius[3] is also stated to have failed to sacrifice at Lavinium before departing for his province in Spain, thereby bringing misfortune upon himself. These incidents point to the meticulous care with which the cult was observed, and the importance which was attached to its preservation among the high magistrates of Rome.

Vesta was also worshipped along with the *Penates* at Lavinium,[4] a fact indicating the Latin origin of her cult; which came to be regarded as the mother-cult[5] of the one observed in the Roman forum. Sacrifice was made to her equally with the *Penates* by the highest officials of Rome. In all likelihood there was a temple sacred to her on the site, but no topographical or other evidence for it has been found, and further discussion of her cult is not within the scope of this work.

The journey from Rome to Lavinium was an accepted and familiar undertaking in the Augustan age as well as all through history. For this purpose alone the road would be kept in some degree of repair, even though the cities were ruinous and the Campagna a wilderness. That Vergil should not at some time have visited the legendary home of the *Penates* and Vesta, the establishment of whose cults on Italian soil play so large a part in Aeneas' divine mission, seems incredible. Could he have gone down to Lavinium in the train of some consul-elect to witness those ancient rites, a few fragments of the scene rise in the imagination. The approach is by the Via Laurentina with a view of the Mediterranean beyond the belt of forest which clothes the road for many miles towards the end of the journey. For the last mile or two the citadel of Lavinium rises above the scene, more majestic on this, the northern side, than on any

---

[1] Servius, *Ad Aen.*, III, 12.

[2] Ascanius, *in Scaurianum*, 21: *crimini dabat sacra publica populi Romani deum Penatium quae Lavini fierent, opera eius minus recte casta fieri.*

[3] Val. Max., I, 67.

[4] Servius, *Ad Aen.*, VII, 150; Macr., *Sat.*, III, 4, 11.

[5] *C.I.L.*, X, 797: and Altheim, *A History of Roman Religion*, translated Mattingly, 1938, pp. 140-1. For Vergil's treatment of the *Penates*, see Cyril Bailey, *Religion in Vergil*, 1935, p. 32 sq. See also an interesting note in Frontinus, *de Coloniis, sub voce* 'Lavinium', which shows a connection with the Vestal Virgins in Imperial times.

PLATE 26. The Rio Torto above Santa Procula (see page 69)

PLATE 27. The Rio Torto below Santa Procula (see page 69)

PLATE 28.   The Rio Torto near the shore (see page 69)

PLATE 29.   Santa Petronella (see page 80)

other. The road ascends the ramp, and turns sharply to the left to enter the area of the acropolis. Here in all probability was the actual home of the *Penates* and their cult, though of the rites and practices observed in their honour we have little knowledge. Here is to be seen the primitive straw hut, their original sanctuary, and, standing beside it, a later temple. In the forum, which is perhaps to the south-west, are the animal bronzes round which so much legend was fabricated, and which must have attracted the attention of many an antiquarian of the time. The rest of the city, once populous, is deserted now and fallen into ruin. Here in this ancient place, Vergil, whose pride was in the traditions of his people, would not fail to recognize one of the oldest memorials of the forefathers of the Latin race which a poet's instinct might inspire, where knowledge could not. The whole picture, so faintly outlined, so wanting in points of light, is one of desolation, in keeping with the words of a later poet:[1]

> *pulvere vix tectae poterunt monstrare ruinae*
> *Albanosque lares Laurentinosque penates*
> *rus vacuum; quod non habitet nisi nocte coacta,*
> *invitus, questusque Numam iussisse, senator.*

[1] Lucan, *Phars.*, VII, 393-6.

F

CHAPTER IV

THE NUMICUS[1]

OF the rivers of the Roman Campagna, the Numicus attracts especial interest, not only because of several ancient cults connected with it and its resultant peculiar sanctity for the Romans, but also because of three references to it in the *Aeneid*. On the day after their landing on the banks of the Tiber, the Trojan comrades prospect the countryside, going out in different directions to learn of the shore, the territory, and the city, of the people to whose land they are come:

> *urbem et finis et litora gentis*
> *diversi explorant.*[2]

They discover that it is the land of the Latins, and that the rivers therein are the Tiber and the Numicus with its marshes:

> *haec fontis stagna Numici,*
> *hunc Thybrim fluvium, hic fortis habitare Latinos.*[3]

These words seem to imply that the Numicus[4] is second in importance only to the Tiber in the newly-discovered land. The mention of the two rivers at this point when the curtain rises on the Trojans' fortunes in Latium, and when after their preliminary sacrifices, the time for action has come, calls to mind the Cumaean Sibyl's prophecy:

> *'bella, horrida bella,*
> *et Thybrim multo spumantem sanguine cerno.*
> *non* Simois *tibi nec* Xanthus *nec Dorica castra*
> *defuerint'.*[5]

The stage is set again as on the plains of Troy, and there are two rivers here to bound the scene as in the former wars.

[1] The substance of this chapter as far as p. 75 was published in *J.R.S.*, 1936, and is reproduced by kind permission of the Council of the Society for the Promotion of Roman Studies.

[2] *Aen.*, VII, 149-50.   [3] *Ibid.*, VII, 150-1.

[4] The precise form of the name is doubtful, the ancient authorities giving either *Numicus* or *Numicius*. Carcopino's opinion is that the form of the name is adjectival in origin, and derived from *numen*, thus indicating a river over which a tutelary god presides. He also points out that in the *Aeneid* it is named only in the genitive case, and so it is not known which form Vergil preferred: *V.O.O.*, 1919, p. 481 and footnote 3.

[5] *Aen.*, VI, 86-9.

The Numicus is again referred to, and in a significant manner when the spokesmen appear before Latinus, and when to the king's question the herald Ilioneus replies:

> *huc repetit iussisque ingentibus urguet Apollo*
> *Tyrrhenum ad Thybrim et fontis vada sacra Numici.*[1]

At this momentous stage in the narrative Vergil may perhaps have wished to make a gesture of reconciliation with another tradition of the Trojan landing which made them first reach Italy on the shore near the Numicus. The linking of the two rivers may be explained here by the poet's acknowledgment of that tradition perhaps too widely accepted to be put lightly aside.[2]

Thirdly in the gathering of the clans, the coastal district of Latium is summarized in the lines:

> *qui saltus, Tiberine, tuos, sacrumque Numici*
> *litus arant Rutulosque exercent vomere collis.*[3]

Apart from the fact that in these passages the Numicus is coupled with the Tiber, and that in the last two its sanctity is manifest, little evidence can be gained from Vergil himself in regard to the actual location of the river. Between Ostia and Antium some half-dozen streams flow over the Roman Campagna and debouch on to the shore of Latium, four of which have severally been recognized by various authorities as the Numicus. About two kilometres south of the Tiber is the Canale dello Stagno (pl. 22), a sluggish stream which serves as a drainage canal for the tract of land, now reclaimed for tillage and pasture, which once was the Ostian lake and the site of ancient salt-beds.[4] It appears originally to have been natural, but at some period to have been canalized as its name suggests; for the course is not quite straight, yet the banks are trim and regular. It is wide enough to admit of a bridge with three arches. After a course skirting the pine woods of Castel Fusano, at most of three kilometres, it enters the sea at the southern end of the modern Roman *lido*, Marina di Ostia. In Roman times its course was shorter by at least six hundred

---

[1] *Aen.*, VII, 241-2.
[2] Dion. Hal., *A.R.*, I, 45; Dio Cassius, fr. 3; Tzetz, *Lyc.*, 1232; Zonaras, VII, 1; See also Boas, *Aeneas' Arrival in Latium, Allard Pierson Stichting, Archaeologisch-Historiche Bydragen*, VI, 1938, p. 53; and also below, p. 1 sq.
[3] *Aen.*, VII, 797-8.   [4] See above, p. 13.

metres; for the line of the sea coast is continually advancing owing to the silting up at the mouth of the Tiber.[1]

Some fifteen kilometres farther south runs the next stream of any importance, Fosso di Pratica, which rises slightly to the east of Pratica di Mare, the ancient Lavinium, and half encircles the acropolis on the north side. The deep-cut valley and the steep side of the acropolis appear to be the result of the river's erosion. Immediately to the west of the city it is joined by the small Rivo di Petronella, which flows down a deep, pleasantly wooded, lateral valley, at the head of which is a natural acropolis, isolated on all sides, and crowned by the farmstead of Santa Petronella. The combined stream then passes under the road leading from Pratica to Rome. This is now called the Via di Decima but it follows in part the lines of two ancient roads leading to Rome.[2] The stream enters the sea about four kilometres farther west (pl. 23). The Fosso is of no great length or size and is of very small volume. It was identified by Cluverius as the Numicus,[3] because he assumed from the ancient evidence that it was the stream that ran by Lavinium, and although the proper location of the city was not known in his day, he did not err very far in placing it at Santa Petronella. At a small distance south of Pratica flows Fosso della Crocetta, a stream of no considerable size and of no geographical or strategic importance. Ardea is situated ten kilometres south of Pratica, bounded by two streams which run past the acropolis and the extensions of the ancient city: Fosso della Molina (or Mola) on the north and Aquabuona on the south. The former is the outlet of Lake Nemi,[4] as was clearly proved by its increased volume during the recent drainage operations. Owing apparently to a false idea of the derivation of the name, the Numicus was once thought by some to have been so called because it was the outlet of Nemi,[5] and so was identified with this river of Ardea. There seems, however, to be no real ground for such an argument.[6] The

[1] See above, p. 4 sq. This canal, or perhaps the salt marshes which it drains, was identified as the Numicus by Bonstetten, *Voyage dans le Latium*, 1805[1], p. 85 sq.

[2] Boëthius, *Roma*, IX, 1931, p. 49 sq.

[3] P. Cluverius, *Italia Antiqua*, III, 1624, p. 894.

[4] Perrone, *Carta idrografica d'Italia*, no.⁰ 26 bis, Tevere[2], 1908, 286.

[5] Volpi, *Vetus Latium Profanum*, XII, 1734, p. 236; a less probable derivation is from *numen*.

[6] Volpi, *ibid.*, XX, p. 81: Pirro Ligorio is quoted as having thought that the Rio Torto flowed out of Nemi.

two rivers meet on the immediate west of Ardea to form the
Fosso dell' Incastro (pl. 24). Its volume is large compared
with the other streams of the Campagna, and considerable
enough to have been navigable in antiquity for small rowboats
for a distance of about two kilometres.[1] The name is thought
to preserve that of the ancient port of Ardea, Castrum Invi.[2]
Ashby was inclined to regard this as the Numicus.[3]

Roughly midway between Ardea and Lavinium flows Rio
Torto, a stream of greater length than any of the others mentioned. It rises under the Alban hills, and, as its name suggests,
takes a winding course of about eighteen kilometres across the
whole width of the Campagna, covering what, in a straight line,
would be a distance of only eleven. Compared with the Fosso
dell' Incastro its width and volume are somewhat small, but the
latter is very variable, and apt to swell suddenly after storms
so that the river becomes wide and dangerous. Nibby has an
interesting passage:[4]

> 'I have obtained information from all the peasants, in
> different years, and they have repeatedly assured me that
> this river swells considerably when there are storms, and
> so rapidly that scarcely a year passes but that some victim
> is mourned who, misled by its customary small volume,
> takes the risk of crossing it on horseback. There are clear
> signs on its banks of the height which the water reaches,
> and of its violence, in the twisted trees that grow along its
> course.'

It crosses the modern so-called Via Laurentina (which, roughly
following the line of the ancient Ardeatina, leads to Ardea) at
Santa Procula (pl. 25). Until recent years, when the drainage
operations were carried out, it formed a wide morass near the
sea, which was full in the rainy season, but which diminished
considerably in summer[5] (pl. 28).

All the rivers of the Campagna, except the Canale dello
Stagno, have certain characteristics in common. The soil is
very soft and absorbent, being composed of three strata: the

---

[1] This statement is made on the verbal authority of Professor Axel Boëthius.
[2] See above, pp. 34-5.
[3] Ashby, *The Roman Campagna in Classical Times*, 1927, p. 217.
[4] Nibby, *Analisi della Carta dei Dintorni di Roma*, vol. II, 1848[2], p. 420. In one
account of the deification of Aeneas he was thought to have been drowned in the river
which was swollen after a sudden storm; see below, p. 79.
[5] Nibby, *ibid.*, p. 419.

first is of vegetable earth, produced by erosion and volcanic detritus, the second of tufa interspersed with lava, and the third of disintegrated rock. The result is that erosion takes place down to the harder strata, and the beds are narrow and very deeply cut, with steeply sloping sides, so that there is an appearance of canalization (pls. 26 and 27). Further, there are *stagna* at the mouth of each, formed by the gathering of water on the land that lies low behind the sand-dunes that fringe the shore (pl. 28). In remote antiquity these inland stretches of water, accessible as they are from the sea, may have afforded safe harbourage for small ships. In the case of Rio Torto the marshes and lagoons are especially clear on the most modern maps of the Campagna, those issued by the Istituto Geografico Militare,[1] and *stagna* are marked at many points along the coast between Ostia and Ardea on most maps of the Campagna. Since they are shown on those dating as far back as 1766,[2] perhaps it is safe to infer that they have always existed.

Most authorities have been in agreement in identifying the Numicus with the Rio Torto, but, as this generally accepted identification has in recent years been challenged, perhaps a restatement of the case may be desirable. Carcopino[3] has been at pains to prove that the Numicus of the *Aeneid* is the Canale dello Stagno. Its history, briefly told, is as follows. In these days it is the chief emissary of the drainage system whereby the land formerly covered by the Ostian lake was reclaimed for tillage and pasture about the year 1873. In ancient times, on the other hand, it must have conducted the salt water to the old salt-beds which are known to have been worked there before those on the right bank of the Tiber. A passage in Livy[4] makes it clear that the early communities on the hills of Rome obtained their salt from beds near the site of Ostia, for the foundation is ascribed to Ancus Martius: 'Silva Maesia Veientibus adempta, usque ad mare imperium prolatum, et in ore Tiberis Ostia urbs condita, salinae circa factae.' Another passage from Festus[5] states that they were known as 'Quiritium Fossae'. As Carcopino points out, there is no evidence what-

---

[1] Istituto Geografico Militare, Fo 158, IV, *N.O.*
[2] Antonio Vallardi.
[3] The following passage is a summary of *V.O.O.*, 1919, pp. 468-91.
[4] Livy, I, 33, 9; also Florus, I, 4; Pliny, *N.H.*, XXXI, 89; Aur. Vict., *De Vir. Ill*, V.
[5] Festus, p. 254 M., 304, Lindsay.

ever, epigraphical or otherwise, to prove that these beds were
used under the Republic or Empire, although their early
existence is vouched for by the name of the Via Salaria, one of
the oldest Roman roads which lead down the left bank of the
Tiber, and was the route by which the Sabines obtained their
supplies of salt.[1] After the conquest of the cities of southern
Etruria, however, in the fourth century B.C., the Romans
worked the salt-beds on the right bank of the Tiber,[2] and then
those fed by the Canale dello Stagno must have reverted to
stagnant salt marshes, and in that condition must they have
been known to Vergil. If proof is needed that the Canale
existed in Roman times,[3] it is to be found in the inscription
which was unearthed near the modern bridge (pl. 22), record-
ing the repairing of a bridge in A.D. 283.[4] A noteworthy point
is that the ditches connecting with the Canale dello Stagno
may in antiquity have had an outlet into the Tiber, just as the
main ditch of the modern drainage system connects both with
the Tiber and the Canale.

Carcopino bases his location of the Numicus on the testimony of Vergil's words *sacer* and *stagnum*, and on the fact
that it is closely coupled with the Tiber in the three references
in the *Aeneid*. Firstly, since in his opinion the name itself is
derived from *numen*, it signifies a sacred river, and need not be
confined to one special stream: in fact, his footnote on page 403
(*op. cit.*) can only be interpreted in this way, for he says, 'Le
Numicus où Numicius de Lavinium ne peut être que le Fosso
de Pratica actuel'. He assumes the Ostian lake to have been
sacred because it is enumerated in a list of sanctuaries which
were struck by lightning in 209 B.C., for which an expiatory
sacrifice was offered.[5] Furthermore, just as the Canale dello
Stagno is not a veritable river, so Vergil styles the Numicus a
fons, with the *stagna*, which are to be recognized in the salt
marshes. Servius[6] states that water from the Numicus was

[1] Festus, p. 326 M., 436, Lindsay.
[2] Livy, VII, 17, 6.
[3] In telling of a project of filling up the marshes in the time of Nero, with rubbish
from the burning of Rome, Tacitus describes them as '*Ostiensis paludes*': *Ann.*, XV, 43.
[4] *C.I.L.*, XIV, 126.   [5] Livy, XXVII, 11, 1-2.
[6] *Ad Aen.*, VII, 150. If the location of the Numicus had been forgotten by the
fourth century A.D., when Servius wrote, then the myth telling of the drying up of the
stream is perhaps aetiological, made up to explain its loss. On the other hand the notice
may be a faithful record of some drainage undertaking along the swampy coastline,
in an attempt to reduce the *stagna*.

used in the worship of Vesta, and from this Carcopino would infer (without, however, any additional proof) that the Vestal Virgins went yearly down from Rome to the marshes of Ostia to obtain salt for their sacrifices. He considers, too, that Servius' obscure statement in the same passage describes the workings of the old salt-beds: 'ista [stagna Numici] iam ab incolis discuntur. quod autem ait stagna verum est: nam Numicus ingens ante fluvius fuit, in quo repertum est cadaver Aeneae et consecratum. post paulatim decrescens in fontem redactus est, qui et ipse siccatus est sacris interceptis'. Lastly Vergil speaks of the two rivers in such close conjunction because the Numicus was in fact connected by the *fossae* of the salt-beds with the Tiber.

Since certain notices from ancient authors support the identification of the Numicus with the Rio Torto, Carcopino considers that Vergil broke away from tradition in identifying it with the outlet of the Ostian lake. Among these notices, perhaps the most valuable is Pliny's list of places lying on the coast of Latium between the Tiber and Antium: 'oppidum Laurentum, lucus Iovis Indigetis, amnis Numicius, Ardea'.[1] The direction followed is from north to south, and on the strength of this alone, Carcopino's[2] theory could be disposed of. According to him, Pliny's expression means the 'town of the Laurentes' and signifies Lavinium. Another more recent interpretation is that of Bendz,[3] who suggests that the *lucus* signifies Lavinium.[4] Both these interpretations must necessarily cause the Numicus to be located between Lavinium and Ardea, that is, where the Rio Torto now flows. It is also possible to maintain that Pliny refers to the Vicus Augustanus Laurentum, the ruins of which lie on the Via Severiana ten kilometres south of the Tiber,[5] and thus to argue for either the Fosso di Pratica or the Rio Torto. Whichever of these possibilities is right, if Pliny's statement be accepted, the Numicus cannot be the Canale dello Stagno.

Carcopino does not attach much importance to Pliny or to certain other writers. There was a legend that Anna, the sister

---

[1] *N.H.*, III, 56. See below, p. 101, for a discussion of Pliny's *Laurentum*.
[2] Carcopino, *V.O.O.*, *livre* II.
[3] Bendz, *Opuscula Archaeologica*, 1934, I¹, pp. 60-1.
[4] The modern name of Pratica, known in the Middle Ages as Patrica, is thought to be derived from *Pater Indiges*. See Carcopino, *V.O.O.*, 1919, pp. 177-8
[5] Dessau, *C.I.L.*, XIV, 2040 sq.; Carcopino, *V.O.O.*, 1919, p. 183.

of Dido, fled for refuge to Latium from Carthage, and was kindly received by Aeneas at Lavinium. She was warned by the shade of Dido, however, to flee from the wrath of Lavinia. In the words of Silius Italicus:

> *'haud procul hinc parvo descendens fonte Numicus*
> *labitur et leni per valles volvitur amne.*
> *huc rapies, germana, viam tutosque receptus'.*[1]

Accordingly, she fled to the Numicus, over the flat pastures of the Campagna:

> *per patulos currit plantis pernicibus agros*
> *donec arenoso, sic fama, Numicius illam*
> *suscepit gremio vitreisque abscondidit antris,*[2]

plunged into its waters and was changed into a nymph. Her pursuers followed her even to the territory of the Rutuli,

> *Rutulum magno errantes clamore per agrum*
> *vicini ad ripas fluvii manifesta sequuntur*
> *signa pedum.*[3]

In its winding course the Rio Torto takes a northern bend which brings it only about three kilometres away from Lavinium. The description of the winding river, the short distance implied, and the mention of the Rutuli leave no doubt that the river was the one which flows between Lavinium and Ardea — was, in fact, the same as the Rio Torto. Ovid's account of the same legend is in accord with the above,[4] and that of the deification of Aeneas gives a corroborating detail that the Numicus debouched on to the Laurentian shore:

> *litus adit Laurens, ubi tectus arundine serpit*
> *in freta flumineis vicina Numicius undis.*[5]

The various accounts of the legendary battle which took place between Mezentius and Aeneas on the banks of the Numicus near the *stagna* after the time when Aeneas was settled in Lavinium, and during which he was drowned, or miraculously disappeared in the river (to be deified and worshipped thereafter as *Pater Indiges*), give some details of topography. Dionysius of Halicarnassus speaks of the great battle which

---

[1] Sil. It., VIII, 179-81.   [2] *Ibid.*, 189-91.   [3] *Ibid.*, 194-6.
[4] Ovid, *Fasti*, III, 523-656.   [5] *Ibid.*, *Met.*, 598-9.

took place not far from Lavinium, saying: 'μάχης δὲ γενομένης καρτερᾶς οὐ πρόσω τοῦ Λαουινίου',[1] 'a great battle taking place not far from Lavinium'. In another account Aeneas is said to have placed his camp 'sub Lavinio', and to have led his troops forth 'circa Numici fluminis stagnum'.[2] These details show a general agreement that the Numicus was near, but not actually at, Lavinium, and further, since Mezentius was the ally of Turnus, that it lay in the strategically important area between Lavinium and Ardea. The story is traced back to Cato by Servius[3] in a passage where he states that the battle took place 'iuxta Laurolavinium'. Thus again the evidence points to the Rio Torto. The legend is also mentioned by Livy,[4] who makes use of the expression 'super Numicum flumen', as does Servius, and almost the same phrase is found in Aurelius Victor — 'super Numici ripam'. The word 'super' suggests the deep-cut beds of the rivers of the Campagna, and would apply well to the Rio Torto, though not in the least degree to the Canale dello Stagno.

The details given with both the flight of Anna, and the battle, suggest also that the river acted as the boundary between the territories of Lavinium and Ardea. This is, perhaps, supported by the evidence of a marble tablet found at Pratica in 1867, and bearing a fragmentary inscription:[5]

```
. . . . . .NVMICE LAVINAS
. . . . v]IRECTA PILVMNI
. . . pon]TIFEX SACRIS VOTVM
. . . . c]LARA SANGVIS AENAE
. . . . m]AXIMVS PETITORVM
. . . . p]ROSPERETIS EVENTVS
. . . . . i]VRA LAVRENTVM
```

As far as these words can be interpreted they seem to record an agreement between Ardea and Lavinium, referring to the boundary in the shape of the river, and the sacred grove of Pilumnus. Although the epithet 'Lavinas' might seem to indicate the Fosso di Pratica, as Carcopino himself admits, yet the coupling of the river with the grove in Ardeatine territory

---

[1] Dion. Hal., *A.R.*, I, 64.   [2] Aur. Vict., *De Or. G.R.*, 14, 4.
[3] *Ad Aen.*, VI, 620.   [4] Livy, I, 2.
[5] *C.I.L.*, XIV, 2065. It is not known where the stone is now. The lines are choliambic; the beginning of each is lost.

is against an identification with the Fosso di Pratica, since Pilumnus was the deified father of Turnus, and points to a stream nearer Ardea.

Thus it is seen that the references in ancient writings which give the clearest topographical details leave no doubt that the Rio Torto was in ancient times the Numicus; and though certain doubtful references can on the surface apply equally well to the Fosso di Pratica, yet admittedly they easily fall into line with the others; for there is no great distance between the two rivers, and the Rio Torto is by situation far the more important. In no one instance, however, could any reference to the Canale dello Stagno be recognized.

If the passage in Vergil's 'Gathering of the Clans' be considered:

> qui saltus, Tiberine, tuos, sacrumque Numici
> litus arant,[1]

the testimony it affords provides a complete refutation of Carcopino. The Canale dello Stagno, itself barely three kilometres in length, is bounded on the south by the primeval maritime pine-forest, stretching for miles, known to antiquity as the Silva Laurentina, and on the north by the salt marshes. No appreciable arable land is near. The Rio Torto, on the other hand, flows across the whole Campagna with its pasture land and tilled fields.

The characteristics of the Numicus, identified as the Rio Torto, justify Vergil's words, sacer and stagnum. The latter, as has been seen, lay at the mouth, and though no satisfactory explanation has really yet been found of Servius' obscure passage in which Carcopino[2] would see a description of the workings of the old salt-beds, the words may yet record some half-remembered attempt to drain the swampy land on the shore. Carcopino's attempt to prove that the Ostian lake was sacred seems to be without any real foundation, since in Roman belief any object struck by lightning was by the very fact considered sacred (sacer). It is certainly not borne out by the project under Nero of filling up the marshes with rubbish from the ashes of Rome.[3]

The several ancient cults connected with the river and the stagna caused it to be held in great reverence. The fact that it

[1] Aen., VII, 797-8.   [2] See above p. 71-2.
[3] Tac., Ann., XV, 43: see above p. 71, note 3.

is the *stagna* which are often called sacred shows that the scene of their observance must have been near the marshy land on the Laurentian shore. To Servius[1] we owe an interesting note on the connection of the Ardeatine cult of Juturna with the Numicus; itself an added proof, if more were needed, of the location of the river near Ardea: 'Juturna fons est in Italia saluberrimus iuxta Numicum fluvium, . . . cum enim naturaliter omnis aqua noxia sit extraneorum corporibus, hic omnibus saluberrimus fons est.' Thus we learn that there was a spring of healing water hard by the river Numicus called Juturna, and we cannot doubt that here, in one of its aspects at any rate, her cult was observed. In the tract of country between Rio Torto and Ardea, there are several springs of acid water (*acqua acetosa*), and perhaps the spring Juturna is to be located in one of these. One actually flows into Rio Torto at Santa Procula, which Nibby styles *la sorgente di Giuturna*, 'the spring of Juturna'.[2] Whether he be right or not, certainly the location of the Numicus is a starting-point for the discovery of the *fons*. Gell[3] suggests that the spring would probably be found in the valley called Cerquetello. Without archaeological evidence it is impossible to locate it in one place rather than in another. The peasants of to-day prize this acid water which is impregnated with the minerals of the volcanic rock through which the spring finds its way, and it is natural and conceivable to suppose that the ancients, too, should know it and attribute its virtues to some indwelling spirit. Servius in the same note would derive the *fons Juturna* from *iuvo* because of the water's healing powers, but Altheim has shown that such a derivation is not possible.[4] We may imagine, too, that in such a spring was to be found the primitive origin of the worship of Juturna, a worship perhaps without any temple or monuments, and practised by the pastoral dwellers on the Campagna long before it came to Rome, and found a place in the forum itself.

As the deified sister of Turnus, Juturna takes a part in the events of the closing scenes of the *Aeneid*. When Juno looks down from the Alban Mount upon the city of Latinus and the ranks of Trojans and Laurentians drawn up to witness the

[1] Servius, *Ad Aen.*, XII, 139.
[2] Nibby, *Analisi della Carta dei Dintorni di Roma*, vol. II, 1848², p. 418.
[3] Gell, *Topography of Rome and its Vicinity*, 1846, p. 101.
[4] Altheim, *Grieschiche Götter im alten Rom*, 1930, pp. 10-13.

combat between Aeneas and Turnus, she speaks to the sister
of Turnus, the goddess who has power over standing pools
and sounding rivers:

> *deam stagnis quae fluminibusque sonoris*
> *praesidet*[1]

addressing her as nymph, pride of the streams, 'nympha, decus
fluviorum'.[2] She urges her to intervene on her brother's behalf
in the course which events are taking.

While Latinus and Aeneas are making the sacrifices which
bind their oaths to abide by the issue of the single combat, the
Rutuli begin to realize that Turnus is ill-matched against
Aeneas. Juturna in the guise of the warrior Camers rouses in
them a desire for a general encounter; and to incite them further
she sends an omen in the form of an eagle which, swooping
down to the river, carries off a goodly swan from among the
flocks of sea birds, which were gathered there, but it is attacked
by the other birds, forced to drop its prey, and at length it is
driven off. The augur Tolumnius interprets this to mean the
defeat of Aeneas and begins the battle. In the midst of all the
fighting Aeneas pursues Turnus, but Juturna, disguised now
as Metiscus, drives his chariot hither and thither, like a
swallow's flight, so that for the time being he escapes.

At length the city itself is attacked, and in despair Amata
hangs herself, thinking that Turnus and together with him all
else is lost. At this moment Juturna in vain tries to divert her
brother's attention from the strife which is raging round the
city, and, though she is still in the likeness of Camers, he recognizes her. In spite of her entreaties he tells her that he realizes
now his duty and is ready to die. Then at last the two champions meet in single combat, and Juturna brings to Turnus his
own strong sword. While the preliminary encounters are
taking place, a change comes over Juno's feelings, for Jupiter
at last persuades her to cease her hatred, and opposition to the
Trojans' fortunes. Juturna in despair prays for death, which
can never be hers, since she is divine; and, wrapping a grey-
green cloak about her head, in sore distress, hides herself in
the depths of the river,

> *tantum effata caput glauco contexit amictu*
> *multa gemens et se fluvio dea condidit alto.*[3]

---

[1] *Aen.*, XII, 139-40.   [2] *Ibid.*, 142 sq.   [3] *Ibid.*, 885-6.

It is for an Altheim[1] to discuss the origins and character of this cult of Juturna, to theorize about the Etruscan origin of the name, and about the priority in age of this over the well-known cult in the forum at Rome. No memorial of any kind has yet been found in the vicinity which could have any reference, however remote, to the worship of the nymph, as nymph she undoubtedly was, but there may have been a close connection with the worship of Castor and Pollux of whose temple at Ardea we have ample literary evidence.[2] Altheim[3] has pointed out that Juturna is often coupled with them, and especially in the Roman forum where their statues were found in close proximity to the spring sacred to her (*lacus Juturnae*). Religious observance at the latter appears from archaeological evidence to date at least from the first half of the fifth century B.C., for the marble group of the Dioscuri found there belongs to that period.[4]

Vergil, the poet, had a peculiar love for the rustic cults of the countryside, even for the simple and primitive deities of shepherds and countrymen. Maybe he knew where was Juturna's spring beside the Numicus, had tasted perhaps its acid stream, and thought in phantasy of the guardian indwelling nymph. So in the *Aeneid* she appears as the sister of Turnus, prince of Ardea, so too she takes refuge in its waters hard by the Numicus river,[5] a veritable spirit of the water, wrapped in a grey-green cloak, the colour of sedge and water-plants.[6]

Another cult related to the Numicus in antiquity, and closely bound up with the Aeneas-legend, is that of *Pater Indiges*. The worship appears to have been observed in a grove placed by Pliny the Elder next to the river: 'Oppidum Laurentum, lucus Iovis Indigetis, amnis Numicus, Ardea.'[7] Silius Italicus speaks of Anna, the nymph of the Numicus, as

[1] *Grieschiche Götter im alten Rom*, 1930, p. 28 sq.
[2] See above p. 48.
[3] Altheim, *Grieschiche Götter im alten Rom*, 1930, p. 14 sq.
[4] Platner and Ashby, *Topographical Dictionary of Rome*, 1929, p. 312.
[5] Servius, *Ad Aen.*, XII, 139, adds that water used to be taken to Rome from the spring for sacrificial purposes. He is, however, probably confusing it with the *lacus Juturnae* in the Roman forum. Altheim, *Grieschiche Götter im alten Rom*, 1930, p. 14 sq., considers that the Ardeatine cult was prior to that of Rome, as does Ward Fowler, *Religious Experience of the Roman People*, 1911, pp. 284-5.
[6] C. Bailey, *Religion in Vergil*, 1934, p. 36, suggests that Vergil represents an older and wider view of the spirit who was worshipped in historical times at the *lacus Juturnae*.
[7] Pliny, *N.H.*, III, 56.

Indigetis castis contermina lucis.[1]

and Dionysius of Halicarnassus, who was in Rome from about 29 B.C. to 7 B.C., has valuable evidence to give, for he saw a *heroon*, which was perhaps the temple, on the banks of the river, planted around with trees, and an inscription which he records as, Πατρός θεοῦ χθονίου ὅς ποταμοῦ Νομικίου ῥεῦμα διέπει'.[2] This may perhaps be translated into Latin as, 'Patris Dei Indigetis, qui Numici amnis undas temperat', and in English is perhaps to be rendered as: '[dedicated to] Pater Indiges who controls the waters of the river Numicus'. That the Roman consuls used to go yearly to make sacrifice in the temple is known from a scholiast on Vergil,[3] and that the cult had some notoriety as late as the third century A.D. is to be concluded from Arnobius' scornful remark, 'Indigetes illi qui in flumen repunt et in alveis Numici cum ranis et pisciculis degunt',[4] 'those Indigetes who creep into the river, and pass their lives with frogs and little fishes'. This deity became incorporated in the Aeneas cycle, and was recognized as Aeneas himself, deified after the battle against Mezentius in which, according to different authorities,[5] he was either slain or drowned in the river swollen after a sudden storm, or miraculously disappeared, only to reappear as the *Indiges*. Ovid, telling how Venus came to the Laurentian shore, and made Aeneas a god by washing away in the river all his mortality, makes an interesting statement proving that the cult was observed by the Romans:

> *contigit os, fecitque deum, quem turba Quiritum*
> *nuncupat Indigetem, temploque arisque recepit.*[6]

The origin of *Pater Indiges*, whoever, or whatever, he was, must be sought in an age far anterior to the time when the legends connected with the Trojans in Italy were popularized;

---

[1] Sil. It., VIII, 39.
[2] Dion. Hal., *A.R.*, I, 64.
[3] Schol. Ver., *Ad Aen.*, I, 260: *Ascanius hostibus devictis in loco quo pater apparuerat Aeneae Indigeti templum dicavit, ad quod pontifices quotannis cum consulibus veniunt sacrificaturi.*
[4] Arnobius, *Ad Nationes*, I, 36.
[5] Dion. Hal., *A.R.*, I, 64; Aur. Vict., *De Or. G.R.*, 14, 4.; Servius, *Ad Aen.*, IV, 620; Solinus, *apud Volp. Vetus Latium Profanum*, 1934, XII, p. 236; Livy, I, 2; Tib. II, 5, 39 sq. The *heroon* has been thought by some to have been the tomb of Aeneas.
[6] Ovid, *Met.*, XIV, 607-8.

the full significance, however, of Vergil's references to the river in the seventh *Aeneid* must have been appreciable to Roman circles: the Numicus was as well known to them as the place of the worship of the *Indiges*, as was Ardea as the centre of the Latin federal cults, and Lavinium for the rites of the *Penates*.

The river is also said to have provided water for the cult of Vesta:[1] some authorities have tried to refer this to the worship of Vesta in the Roman forum, but the distance makes this impossible. The reference can only be to that observed at Lavinium in connection with the cult of the *Penates*.[2]

EXCURSUS ON THE SUPPOSED SITE OF A TEMPLE
DEDICATED TO ANNA PERENNA

The cult of Anna Perenna is worthy of further consideration, for its apparent connection with the Numicus has caused some writers to place the river at Lavinium. At Castel di Leva, which lies in the north-west angle of the junction of the modern so-called Via Laurentina, and that of the road from Albano to Pratica di Mare, is a small, pleasantly wooded, sunken valley which runs down to the Via di Decima and skirts the north-west side of the acropolis of Lavinium. At the head of this valley, where it is at its widest, there stands a small, conical-shaped hill, isolated on all sides. It is called Santa Petronella, and on the summit stands a fairly large farmhouse of the same name. On the eastern side a gentle slope leads to the top, but on all other sides the ground is almost precipitous (pl. 29). Incorporated in the buildings is an old chapel dedicated to the woman saint, but now used as a barn. The walls are white-washed and nothing remains to show its former sanctity but a niche in the farthest wall which once probably held an image. The inhabitants, to the writer's surprise, knew that this had once been a *capella* or chapel, and were pleased to show it.

This chapel was seen by Bonstetten[3] during his travels over the Campagna in 1819, and in his enthusiasm for discovering

---

[1] Servius, *Ad Aen.*, VII, 150: *Vestae enim libari non nisi hoc fonte licebat*; Macr., *Sat.*, II, 4, 11.

[2] See above, pp. 63-4 sq.

[3] Bonstetten, *Voyage dans le Latium*, 1861², pp. 193-204. The *Acta Sanctorum* 1756, May, IV, p. 769 sq., give no evidence for the name of Anna.

PLATE 30. General view of Zolforata, showing a sulphur deposit in the
foreground, and the Alban Mount in the background (see page 105)

PLATE 31. Disused sulphur mines (see page 106)

PLATE 33. Cave containing sulphur spring, possibly to be identified as the 'Grotto of Albunea'

(see page 108)

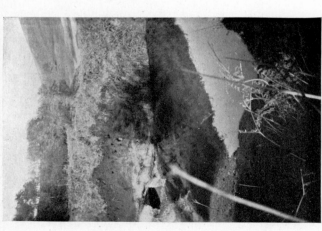

PLATE 32. Disused sulphur mine formerly identified as the 'Grotto of Albunea'

(see page 106)

Vergilian and other sites, unreasonably adding the name of Anna to that of Petronella, concluded that the shrine was the fane of Anna Perenna, now become a Christian saint. The *Fasti Vaticani*,[1] however, make it clear that the festival of the ancient, rustic goddess took place in Rome, on the Ides of March, at the first milestone on the Via Flaminia, that is, in the *Campus Martius*, near the modern Porta del Pópulo.[2] The place and date of it are vouched for by Ovid,

> *Idibus est Annae festum geniale Perennae,*
> *Non procul a ripis, advena Thybri, tuis.*[3]

Martial, too, states that her grove could be seen from the Ianiculum at a point between the Via Flaminia and the Via Salaria.[4] It was, perhaps, somewhere in what is now the Borghese Gardens. Seeing that the cult was rustic, only observed by the *plebs*[5] and that a grove (*nemus*) was the shrine of the goddess, it is very unlikely that there was a temple connected with it, as most writers have assumed.

Around Anna Perenna, who was perhaps in origin the spirit of the ring or the recurring round of the year,[6] but whose meaning was forgotten in later times, certain aetiological myths sprang up, the chief one of which connects her with the Numicus. She was thought to have been that Anna, the sister of Dido, who, fleeing for refuge into the *stagna* of the Numicus, became a nymph. The character of a water-nymph does not, however, accord with the known details of the cult and its goddess, and thus this identification is seen to be imaginary. The story is only one of several concerning her, and, to use Warde Fowler's words, 'It is probable that she only came into connection with the Numicus because Aeneas was there already'. Since here is an example of an old cult on which was superimposed a story fabricated in an age when the Aeneas cycle of legend was popular, it is probably unsafe to assume that the festival was observed on the banks of the Numicus as well as at Rome.

[1] *C.I.L.*, I, 1, 311: *Feriae Annae Perennae, Via Flaminia, ad lapidem primum.*
[2] Warde Fowler, *Roman Festivals*, 1899, p. 50, footnote 4.
[3] Ovid, *Fasti*, III, 523-4: the second line cannot be taken to refer to the Numicus which is at least twenty kilometres away.
[4] Martial, IV, 64, 17.
[5] See Ovid for details of the cult, *Fasti*, III, 523 sq. He gives a fanciful derivation of her name: *amne perenne latens, Anna Perenna vocor.*
[6] Warde Fowler, *Roman Festivals*, 1899, p. 52.

G

Furthermore, a genuine saint, by name Petronilla,[1] was buried in the catacombs of Domitilla, a mile and a half from Rome, near the ancient Via Ardeatina, together with Saints Nero and Achilles. These catacombs are entered from an upper church of the fourth century dedicated to her, and in them can be seen in a small side chapel a fresco of the same century depicting the saint and inscribed with her name. It is not then remarkable that farther down the same road (for the present Via Laurentina corresponds to the old Via Ardeatina) should exist a small shrine sacred to her. When, too, it is noted that her festival does not coincide with that of Anna Perenna, but falls on May 31st, the relation between the two is seen to be fictitious. In fact, the supposed connection of Anna Perenna[2] with the Numicus seems to fade out under close examination, and even if it ever had any real existence, it cannot, in our state of knowledge, afford any topographical evidence at all.

[1] *Acta Sanctorum*, 1756, May, IV, p. 769.

[2] Peronilla is found as a form of Petronilla as early as 1330. Nibby, *Analisi della Carta dei Dintorni di Roma*, vol. II, 1848², p. 559, and even Perrine *Acta Sanctorum, ibid.*, which seems to have been added reason for connecting the goddess with the saint.

CHAPTER V

VERGIL'S LAURENTUM

hinc vasta palus, hinc ardua moenia cingunt.[1]

THERE seems to be no reasonable doubt that an ancient settlement called Laurentum, dating from such early beginnings as those of Ardea and Lavinium, once existed, not only because of the literary tradition, but also because of the name of the Via Laurentina.[2] It would appear from this that ancient Laurentum was nearer Rome than Lavinium,[3] but that the name of the road was retained even after prolongation to Lavinium and the coast, both because the shore in that neighbourhood was known as Laurentum, and because in the greater part of its length it served the *ager Laurens*. It is the writer's intention to show that the site of this ancient settlement was so early lost, perhaps in early historic times, that it cannot be considered to be the Laurentum of the *Aeneid*, but that the Laurentum of Vergil's time was in fact a cult centre near the Numicus and the Laurentian shore. The monuments existing in that neighbourhood were comparable with what then remained at Ardea and Lavinium, and led the poet with his contemporaries to recognize there traces of an ancient city with characteristic temple sites and cult survivals, and to give it place in the *Aeneid* transformed by touches of epic splendour into the city of Latinus, a city having an *arx* crowned by the king's palace, and ennobled by memorials of his ancient line.

The ancient records are both confused and confusing, both because, although the old lost town of Laurentum probably never advanced beyond the status of an early Latian settlement, it is styled *urbs* and πόλις by the historians through literary exaggeration, and also because several places on the Campagna were known as Laurentum: that of the Itineraries[4] for instance

---

[1] *Aen.* XII, 745.

[2] Ashby, *Classical Topography of the Roman Campagna*, vol. I, p. 127, has shown that local roads took their names from the cities they served. The Via Latina and the Via Salaria seem to be the only exceptions. For the latter, see above, p. 13.

[3] Ashby, *ibid.*, p. 128. A close comparison may be made with the Via Praenestina. This originally only went as far as Gabii, and was therefore known as the Via Gabina until it was extended to Praeneste. Livy, II, 11, 7; III, 6, 7; V, 49, 6.

[4] *Antonine Itinerary*, ed. Cuntz, Leipzig, 1929, 301: *Carta Peutingeriana*. The distance given as sixteen miles from Rome is correct for the *Vicus*.

is undoubtedly the Vicus Augustanus Laurentum, a small village situated at the modern Grotto di Piastra on the Via Severiana about ten kilometres south of Ostia. Since Dessau[1] has shown from a study of the excavations and inscriptions that this was a foundation of Augustus, it is too late to have had any place in the Aeneas-legend: it is unlikely therefore that any literary notice of Laurentum connected with the *Aeneid* or the legends has reference to this Vicus. In this neighbourhood, too, there were later Imperial villas of the name Laurentum.[2]

So far scholars in their researches have not separated the lost early settlement from Vergil's Laurentum, and this has made for further confusion. No less than seven different places have been identified as a 'prétendue Laurente',[3] and the most recent investigation ends in the conclusion that Laurentum lay in the neighbourhood of Capocotta.[4] These writers all sought to locate a city supposedly belonging to primitive times and comparable with Ardea and Lavinium; yet not one of the sites chosen suits the geographical and defensive needs of an early Latian settlement, conditions which must be fulfilled in any sure identification. In contrast with all attempts to locate a site, there is the view formed by Carcopino,[5] and reached just before him by Dessau,[6] that Lavinium alone existed and bore the name of Laurentum until she was founded for a second time by Aeneas, when he married Lavinia, and took over the government from Latinus. Carcopino has substantiated his theory by minute and detailed argument, the particulars of which need not be given here. It has found a strong following among classical scholars of whom especially may be mentioned Wissowa, Beloch, Frazer, Ashby, and Saunders.

At the outset of our inquiry we may not assume that the name of Laurentum in every case indicates an actual *city*, but

---

[1] Dessau, *C.I.L.*, XIV, pp. 185 and 486. His date is accepted by Carcopino, *V.O.O.*, 1919, p. 183. It may be the *colonia Ostiensis* of Pliny's letter, *Ep.* II, 17, 27.

[2] Dessau, *ibid*. Pliny's villa was in the vicinity, *Ep.* II, 17, 1.

[3] For the references see Carcopino, *V.O.O.*, 1919, p. 173; also for more recent theories see Rehm, *Das geographische Bild des alten Italiens in Vergils Aeneis*, 1932; *Philologus Supplementband*, XXIV, Heft II; Bendz, *Opuscula Archaeologica*, I¹, 1934, 62 sq. In a conversation in 1939 Professor G. Lugli was inclined to agree with the writer's suggestion that the lost site might perhaps be found near Decima, on the Via Laurentina, about ten miles from Rome, where the ground presents possibilities.

[4] Bendz, *Opuscula Archaeologica*, I¹, 1934, 62 sq.

[5] Carcopino, *V.O.O.*, 1919, *livre* II.

[6] Dessau, *C.I.L.*, XIV.

we must seek to discover from the ancient authorities what was its significance, especially from those who were contemporaries, or nearly so, of the poet, and who thus reflect the current legends and the same or actual sources upon which he himself drew. It is enough for this inquiry to attempt to discover *Vergil's* conception of the *urbs Latini*, and its appeal to the Romans of his day. Rehm[1] has well summarized the situation when he remarks that Vergil's whole description of the city of the Latins does not rest only on poetic fiction, but that he and his sources doubtless imagined a city, which had an important place in the primitive history of Latium, on a definite site in the *ager Laurens*, even if this was all merely conjecture. The present writer would go further in saying that Vergil's Laurentum must inevitably be a place which had some connection with the Aeneas-legends then popular, and with the religion of the times. It must be remembered that Ardea and Lavinium were known to him, and only existed as little more than centres of cults which had lived on after the cities' decline: it is probable that Vergil's Laurentum was just such a cult centre, for neither the deeply religious nature of the *Aeneid*, nor the poet's preoccupation with the deities of the countryside, must be forgotten.

The name Laurentum[2] occurs many times in the historians, but in only a few instances can it with any certainty be referred to a city. In a passage in Dionysius of Halicarnassus,[3] the two Tarquins are said to come 'ἐκ Λαυρέντου πόλεως', 'from the city of Laurentum'. It might be argued that the Greek means a city of the *ager Laurens*, but on the other hand, if it is taken to mean a city called Laurentum, then here is a valuable statement reflecting a tradition coming from the fifth century B.C. of the former existence of a city[4] so-called. A late writer, Lydus,[5] tells how Aeneas landed 'ἐν πόλει τῆς 'Ιταλίας λεγομένη Λαυρεντία': 'at a city of Italy called Laurentia' (that is, Laurentum). The source of this statement is probably to be attributed

---

[1] Rehm, *Das geographische Bild des alten Italiens in Vergils Aeneis*, 1932; *Philologus Supplementband*, XXIV, Heft II, p. 55.

[2] Λαύρεντον or Λώρεντον in the Greek: the two forms appear to be used indiscriminately.

[3] Dion. Hal., *A.R.*, V, 54, 1.

[4] The site was so early lost that it probably never reached the real status of a city: tradition probably exaggerated its importance and caused the Greek historians to style it πόλις (city).

[5] Lydus, *De Mens.*, I, 13.

to Aristotle since a passage in Dionysius of Halicarnassus,[1] apparently its parallel, is acknowledged by the author as coming from him. If this passage is to be regarded as acceptable, then its antiquity is significant and causes it to fall into line with the other ancient records which appear to give testimony of the old tradition of a city called Laurentum. Livy speaks of a city, the dwelling-place of Latins, of which he does not give the name, but probably leaves it to be inferred from that of the *ager*: 'Laurentum agrum tenuisse . . . Latinus rex aboriginesque . . . ex urbe atque agris concurrunt.'[2]

Against Carcopino's theory, that Laurentum and Lavinium were not two separate cities, two records can be quoted. In Plutarch's account of the murder of Titus Tatius at Lavinium, envoys are said to have come 'ἀπὸ Λαυρέντου', 'from Laurentum', and the murder is stated to have taken place 'ἐν Λαβινίῳ', 'at Lavinium'.[3] Furthermore, Dionysius gives a list of thirty peoples united in the treaty of Cassius, the *foedus Cassianum*, among them both the Laurentes and Lavinates.[4] Scholars, however, at present are not prepared to accept this as a historical document,[5] and so perhaps too much importance must not be attached to it at present.

The most valuable notice of all, both for the tradition of a former 'city', and for its separate existence from Lavinium, is to be found in a quotation from Cato's *Origines* preserved by Servius:[6] 'Cato enim in Originibus dicit Troianos a Latino accepisse agrum qui est inter Laurentum et Castra Troiana.' 'Cato states in the *Origines* that the Trojans received land which is between Laurentum and Castra Troiana.' The antiquity of this excerpt belonging to the second century B.C. increases its importance. Those who believe that a city called Laurentum never existed would argue that the name refers to the *ager* or the *civitas*.[7] Yet there are clear indications in the *Aeneid* that the *ager* was thought to extend from the bank of the Tiber farther south than Ardea, because both the river

[1] Dion. Hal., *A.R.*, I, 72, 3. *Sub voce* Λωμεντός the late writer, Stephanus of Byzantium, speaks of Laurentum as πόλις 'Ιταλίας, 'a city of Italy', but too much stress must not be laid on a record of so late a date.

[2] Livy, I, 5.

[3] Plut., *Rom.*, XXIII.

[4] Dion. Hal., *A.R.*, V, 61, 3.

[5] The whole question is discussed at length, Carcopino, *V.O.O.*, 1919, p. 228 sq.

[6] *Ad Aen.*, XI, 316.

[7] See especially Carcopino, *V.O.O.*, 1919, p. 196.

Tiber[1] and Turnus[2] are called *Laurens*. It would then be manifestly absurd to hold that the name of Laurentum in Cato's passage stands for the *ager*. Furthermore, we cannot, for the obvious reason of the text itself, maintain that here Laurentum and Lavinium are synonymous, as Carcopino would try to do in instances, such as this, where Laurentum does not refer to the *ager*.

We must now examine other notices where the name occurs with a different significance. In various accounts of the Trojan landing,[3] the beach is styled Laurentum and located near the mouth of the Tiber or that of the Numicus. Dionysius, whose history is so valuable for our inquiry because he came to Rome in 30 B.C., describes the landing-place as not far from the mouth of the Tiber.[4] According to him Laurentum cannot have been very near to the river Tiber, because not only are the Trojans said to be in need of water, but they are furthermore only *about an hour's walk from where Aeneas was later to found Lavinium*.[5] Since Lavinium stands about three kilometres above the shore, for Dionysius the landing-place cannot be far north or south of a point in a direct line with the site of the city. Strabo's account is so nearly in agreement as to suggest that he used the same source:[6] ʽφασὶ δὲ Αἰνείαν μετὰ τοῦ πατρὸς Ἀγχίσου καὶ τοῦ παιδὸς Ἀσκανίου καταράντας εἰς Λαύρεντον τῆς πλησίον τῶν Ὠστίων καὶ τοῦ Τιβέρεως ἠιόνος ... κτίσαι πόλιν', 'they say that Aeneas after landing with his father Anchises and his son Ascanius at Laurentum on the beach near Ostia and the Tiber, founded a city'. His words also do not suggest the actual mouth of the Tiber. If both historian and geographer had meant that the Trojans sailed up the river, they would surely have mentioned Ostia. The words αἰγιαλός in the one, and ἠιών in the other, perhaps only indicate a landing-beach next in order on the sea-board of Latium to the mouth of the river on the south when the whole stretch of coast is visualized, especially, too, since in both narratives the Trojans are described as arriving there from Troy and not from another intermediary place in Italy. Although these two accounts appear to be in agreement as far

[1] *Aen.*, V, 797.   [2] *Ibid.*, VII, 650.
[3] See page 1 sq. and references cited there.
[4] Dion. Hal., *A.R.*, I, 48.
[5] Dion. Hal., *ibid.*, 55, 56. These observations are made by Boas, *Aeneas' Arrival in Latium, Allard Pierson Stichting, Archaeologisch-Historische Bvdragen*, VI, 1938, p. 53.
[6] Strabo, V, 229.

as regards details of the landing, in other respects they differ; Dionysius goes on to describe the founding of Lavinium, but Strabo mentions first the founding of a city which he does not name, also twenty-four stades from the sea, but possibly means by it Troia Nova; later he speaks of the founding of Lavinium near the spot where Aeneas gained a victory over the Rutuli. He thought that Latinus lived on the site of Rome, perhaps with reference to the Loretum[1] on the Aventine, or as a reflection of the oldest tradition which brought Aeneas directly to Rome.[2] By later writers, Laurentum, the landing-place, is located near the Numicus: it is so described both by Dio Cassius[3] and by Zonaras[4] who probably used Dio's history as his source. In the writer's opinion this location need not be considered to be at variance with that of Dionysius and Strabo, but to give added details and to represent another facet of the same tradition. At any rate, the account as given by Dio cannot be a post-Vergilian accretion because no new fabrication would be likely to come into being at variance with the *Aeneid*. Rehm,[5] it is to be noted, points out that the Numicus was near the traditional landing-place and puts the Trojan beach a little to the north of the river. Appian[6] also describes Laurentum as a beach, αἰγιαλός, but gives no topographical indications: he adds that Aeneas' camp was shown there in his day, from which we perhaps may be permitted to understand ruins of some epoch which had become connected in popular belief with the Trojan legend. The two altars which Dionysius[7] says were shown in his day, where the Trojans made a thank-offering for water, perhaps have some relation to the remains mentioned by Appian as having a place in the Trojan myths. All the historians quoted, except Strabo, further agree that the place of the actual disembarkation was called Troia.[8]

---

[1] The ancient grove of laurels on the Aventine: Platner and Ashby, *Topographical Dictionary of Rome*, 1929, *sub voce* 'Loretum'.

[2] Boas, *Aeneas' Arrival in Latium, Allard Pierson Stichting Archaeologisch-Historische Bydragen*, VI, 1938, p. 54 and citations.

[3] Dio Cassius, fr. 3 Tzetz, *Lyc.* 1232.

[4] Zonaras, VII, 1.

[5] Rehm, *Das geographische Bild des alten Italiens in Vergils Aeneis*, 1932; Philologus Supplementband, XXIV, Heft II, p. 44, and map, p. 108.

[6] Appian, I, 1.

[7] Dion. Hal., *A.R.*, I, 55. See above, p. 2.

[8] See 2 sq. above for a discussion of the nature of a *Troia*.

Strabo's[1] Laurentum, enumerated in his geography of Latium as lying between Lavinium and Ardea, clearly refers to some place on this stretch of shore, and we need see no confusion in his two records:[2] 'ἀνὰ μέσον δὲ τούτων τῶν πόλεών [i.e. Ostia and Antium] ἐστι τὸ Λαουίνιον, ... εἶτα Λαύρεντον, ὑπέρκειται δὲ τούτων ἡ 'Αρδέα', 'between these cities is Lavinium, then Laurentum, there lies beyond these, Ardea'. It is self-evident that the geographer first states the names of the coastal towns which bound Latium, Ostia on the north and Antium on the south. Then he returns to the north and enumerates the chief places in their order from north to south. It is quite inconceivable that in such a straightforward statement he should have first described the order from north to south in the case of Ostia and Antium and have reverted to an order south to north before mentioning Ardea. This passage contains an implication that there were ruins connected with cult survivals at Laurentum, seeming to him like traces of a city comparable with those to be seen in his day at both Ardea and Lavinium. The Laurentum mentioned by Cicero where his friends used to gather shells may be recognized, too, as this same stretch of shore.[3] Thus we have evidence from writers of late republican, and Augustan times, and as late as the beginning of the third century A.D., that the stretch of coast south of the Tiber and connected with the Numicus was called Laurentum. It is legitimate to suppose that it was the tract of Latian sea-board lying between these two rivers, and probably not farther south than the Numicus because there lay Ardeatine territory. At some point on this beach, called Troia, the Trojans were thought to have come to land, and ruins lying in the neighbourhood were brought into connection with the legend.[4] This tradition may be regarded as having taken root not only around an indigenous place name,[5] but also around the memory of maritime activity on this coast connected with the early history of the Latian cities, especially Ardea[6] and

[1] Strabo, V, 232.   [2] See above, p. 87.

[3] Cic., De Orat., II, 22: sed tamen ita solet narrare Scaevola, conchas eos et umbilicos ad Caietam et ad Laurentum legere consuesse. Cf. Val. Max., VIII, 8: constat Scipionem et Laetium Caietae et Laurenti vagos litoribus conchulos et umbilicos lectitasse.

[4] The legend of the coming of Anna to the Laurentian shore, as given by Ovid, Fasti, III, 523 sq., also reflects the tradition of a landing-beach near the Numicus.

[5] T. Frank, A.J.P., XLV, 1924, has shown that Troia is a native Italian name. See above, p. 2 sq.

[6] See above, p. 33.

Lavinium, belonging to an epoch earlier than the functioning of Ostia as a port, and every account of such a tradition probably goes back to a source anterior to her founding. We have the express testimony of Polybius for the importance of the Laurentian shore in the late sixth century in his record of the first treaty between Rome and Carthage which is to be dated to 508 or 507 B.C.:[1] ῾Καρχηδόνιοι δὲ μὴ ἀδικέιτωσαν δῆμον ᾽Αρδεατῶν, ᾽Αντιατῶν, Λαρεντίνων, Κιρκαιιτῶν, Ταρρακινιτῶν', 'the Carthaginians are not to molest the people of Ardea, Antium, Laurentum, Circeum, Terracina'. A landing-beach serving the Laurentes would indicate the need for a *castrum* such as the Castrum Invi which served Ardea.[2] Such may be the Laurentum mentioned by Strabo,[3] and the camp mentioned by Appian,[4] connected with the Trojan legend, as lying in ruins.

It is perhaps in the neighbourhood of this beach and the river which debouches on to it, both so closely wrapped in the Aeneas-legend, that we may seek to recognize Vergil's Laurentum. Many scholars have sought to locate a Laurentum on the same volcanic ridge on which stand Ardea and Lavinium, but always to the north of the latter, searching, and rightly if they seek for the early city,[5] for a situation in accord with the needs of a primitive Latin settlement, with an acropolis easily defended, and a site raised above the marshy sea-board. All these are characteristic of both Ardea and Lavinium, and other coastal cities of Latium, and even those of southern Etruria. Their search has so far failed. .

The question of the existence and location of Laurentum has been inevitably bound up in the question of the tracing of the route of the Via Laurentina. This great problem has perhaps been solved in recent years by Boëthius,[6] and has been usefully summarized by him. There were in antiquity six roads which led from Rome across the Campagna to a city, each city having its own road. In the course of time the line of the roads has been lost in places, confused with by-roads incorporated in newer ones, and even wrongly named. These six are the Via di Satricum (so named by modern scholars), the

---

[1] Polyb., III, 22. See also Boëthius, *Roma*, X, 1931, 56; also above, p. 34. A late sixth-century date has been recently reaffirmed by Beaumont, *J.R.S.*, XXIX, 1939, p. 74 sq., who bases his arguments chiefly on the spheres of influence controlled by Carthage in the Mediterranean, and on the fact that there is no reference to Spain.

[2] See above, pp. 34-5.   [3] Strabo, V, 232.   [4] Appian, I, 1, and above, p. 88.
[5] See above, p. 84.   [6] *Roma*, IX, 1931: *Le Strade nel Distretto di Ardea.*

Via Ardeatina (now called Via Laurentina), the ancient Via
Laurentina (the modern Via di Decima), two traced but still
unnamed, and the Via Severiana. One of the unnamed roads
has been traced from Castel di Massimo south to Pizzo Preti,
and thence to Trigoria and Castel Romano. At the latter point
there were two branches, one serving as a by-road to the
Severiana, joining it at Tor Paterno, and to the Vicus Augustanus Laurentum, the other proceeding to Lavinium. This,
however, does not seem to have been a large, systematized
road, though if proof of its antiquity be needed, says Boëthius,
it is enough to walk on the path between Trigoria and Castel
Romano. This road, which can only have been of minor importance, is styled by Boëthius, Via di Lavinio. The actual
Laurentina, the route of which has so long remained doubtful,
is now to be traced as follows: for the first four kilometres it
was identical with the Ostiensis, but branched off from it at
Ponte Fratta, continuing by the *trattoria* of Malpasso, by Castel
di Decima, Capocotta, and arriving at Lavinium, and on the
way passing through the woods of Castel Porziano. To it
belong milestones[1] of the age of Tiberius, showing that it was
a highway either *publica* or *militaris*. Carcopino styled the two
Laurentina Vetus et Nova, and took as one of his main arguments against the existence of Laurentum the fact that the road
went to Lavinium. Neither he nor any scholar, however, seems
to have considered that the Laurentina might have passed
through Lavinium, and continued towards the sea on the south.
The road, however, does appear to leave Lavinium again on
the south, where a path descends the slight incline of the city's
boundary, with a few characteristic paving stones *in situ* at a
level about two feet higher than the present one. This road
leads straight down to the flat land near the *stagna* of the
Numicus, in the direction, that is, of the beach called Laurentum. Lanciani knew of its existence and route, but merely
called it, in his plan of Lavinium, 'Via ad Campum Veneris
Ducens'.[2] A recent writer, Bendz,[3] makes the statement that
Laurentum must have stood *probably in a more advantageous
position than that of Ardea and Lavinium*, and concludes that

---

[1] *C.I.L.*, XIV, 4086 and 4087. Dessau. Castel di Decima is named after the tenth
milestone which is *in situ* on the side of the road.
[2] See plan of Lavinium, p. 56 above.
[3] Bendz, *Opuscula Archaeologica*, I¹, 1934, p. 162.

some place near Capocotta meets the requirements. To one who is familiar with the ground and with the characteristics of the two sites mentioned, such a suggestion is inadmissible. The farmhouse of Capocotta itself stands on what is only a piece of gently rising ground — a mere hillock if the building were removed. On these grounds alone we can reject the place as impossible for the site of an early city of Latium. So far critics and scholars have not sought for Vergil's Laurentum south of Lavinium. Even Bendz, the latest exponent, dismisses the possibility with the sentiment that the action of the *Aeneid* makes it nearer the Tiber, basing his assumption on what is a manifest absurdity: that certain lines at the beginning of the eighth book of the *Aeneid*[1] suggest that Aeneas could see from the Castra Troiana on the bank of the Tiber what was happening in the Latin city! Bendz fails to notice that the line is prefaced by the words 'talia per Latium'! Even at a distance of a mile, on such flat and wooded country this would have been physically impossible; yet he tried to locate the city at Capocotta, at a distance of some fifteen miles away to satisfy the action of the *Aeneid*. It is neither necessary nor reasonable to assume that Laurentum lay to the north of Lavinium.

Another recent location, that of Rehm,[2] places Laurentum at Castel Porziano, a situation which he considers was suited to the action of the *Aeneid*, although untrue in reality. Rehm fails to consider Lanciani's identification of this site with ancient Pomonal, and what is more important, to attempt to discover any connection which the site may have had in the cycle of Trojan legend. Vergil wrote of places well known to his contemporaries in most cases for ancient cults which continued to be observed and held in due reverence. He could not, without violating poetic artistry and without losing prestige as a poet, alter the scene, as Rehm suggests, to fit the action of the epic. The religious nature of the poem, the regard which the poet had for existing cult centres, and the conservatism of Roman religion cannot be ignored in treating of its topography. Carcopino's[3] view that there was in reality only one city, originally called Laurentum, and after a second

[1] *Aen.*, VIII, 19.
[2] Rehm, *Das geographische Bild des alten Italiens in Vergils Aeneis*, 1932; Philologus Supplementband, XXIV, Heft II, p. 50 sq.
[3] Carcopino, *V.O.O.*, *livre* II.

founding by Aeneas receiving the name of Lavinium after his Italian bride, would greatly detract from the dramatic force of the epic. The chief mission of the Trojans is to find and found a new home for the *Penates*: the walls of the new city shall rise for them according to divine promise, and they *themselves* shall build them:

'*mihi moenia Teucri*
constituent urbique dabit Lavinia nomen'.[1]

None of the historians makes any suggestion that Aeneas took over a city already in existence, nor does any record of the legend do so. The Augustan paintings from a house on the Esquiline hill, now in the Terme Museum in Rome, showing a series of scenes from the Trojan cycle, can probably be said to record what was the accepted form of the legend in Vergil's own time. Two of the motifs show the building of city walls; one must therefore represent the founding of Lavinium, and the other that of Alba Longa. In tradition, and poetic conception at least, if not in reality, the city surely had its being, and we may turn now to the epic itself for enlightenment.

In the Sixth *Aeneid* after the pageantry of Roman heroes which passes by Aeneas in the Fields of the Blessed, and after the revelation of the might and greatness of future Rome, Anchises turns to events which immediately await his son in the world of reality. He speaks of imminent wars, and of the people with whom they will be waged, the Laurentians and their city, and Latinus, their king, tells him, too, of the hazards and fortunes of the coming encounter.

exin bella viro memorat quae deinde gerenda,
Laurentisque docet populos urbemque Latini,
et quo quemque modo fugiatque feratque laborem.[2]

These are to be his foes. They have a city and a king, but the city is left nameless, though the name is perhaps to be understood from that of the people. With this prophetic prelude, when on the threshold of Latium, Aeneas is prepared for his entrance into the land of promise. Carcopino has shown that the name of Laurentum is not to be found for a certainty anywhere in the *Aeneid*.[3] Though the name cannot be recognized,

---

[1] *Aen.*, XII, 193-4.　　[2] *Ibid.*, VI, 890-2.
[3] Carcopino, *V.O.O.*, 1919, *livre* II, p. 276. He finds three passages where the name might be recognized; twenty-two containing the epithet *Laurens,* and twenty-eight where the city is mentioned in paraphrase.

it can again be inferred from a hint given later by the poet when he tells of the ancient and sacred laurel tree which grew in the courtyard of Latinus' palace and after which he had named the inhabitants *Laurentes*. The city, too, is to be understood as taking its name from the tree; it is plainly Laurentum.

> *laurus erat tecti medio in penetralibus altis*
> *sacra comam multosque metu servata per annos,*
> *quam pater inventam, primas cum conderet arces,*
> *ipse ferebatur Phoebo sacrasse Latinus,*
> *Laurentisque ab ea nomen posuisse colonis.*[1]

The suspension of names is an acknowledged conceit in ancient epic, characteristic of both Vergil and Homer. The scene, circumstances of the action, and even personages are considered as well known and needing no introduction or explanation.[2] They are often given only at a dramatic moment in the narrative, but it is not inconceivable that in some cases the name need not be given at all.

When Aeneas lands in Latium on the banks of the Tiber he is already, for Vergil, on Laurentian soil, as an earlier passage in the *Aeneid* indicates, in which the epithet of *Laurens* is added to the river.

> *quod superest, oro, liceat dare tuta per undas*
> *vela tibi, liceat Laurentem attingere Thybrim.*[3]

On the day after their landing the Trojans go forth in different directions to make reconnaissance of the territory, the shore, and the city. They return to Aeneas with the news that the river on the bank of which their fleet is drawn up is the Tiber, that there is another called the Numicus, which apparently marks the limit of their search, and that the land is the dwelling-place of the Latins.

> *Postera cum prima lustrabat lampade terras*
> *orta dies, urbem et finis et litora gentis*
> *diversi explorant: haec fontis stagna Numici,*
> *hunc Thybrim fluvium, hic fortis habitare Latinos.*[4]

---

[1] *Aen.*, VII, 59-63.

[2] Boas, *Aeneas' Arrival in Latium, Allard Pierson Stichting, Archaeologisch-Historiche Bydragen*, VI, 1938, pp. 82-3: 'This was according to Vergil's own artistic intentions ... a restriction of all that was not strictly necessary, to enhance the loftiness of the epic, to retain the broad outline.'

[3] *Aen.*, V, 796-7.   [4] *Ibid.*, VII, 148-51.

As has already been shown,[1] the Numicus is that river now called the Rio Torto, which flows into the sea some sixteen miles south of the Tiber, and the *stagna* are the lagoons which lay near the mouth, behind the sand dunes. The discovery of the two rivers brings fulfilment of the Cumaean Sibyl's prophecy[2] that the scene of Troy is to be laid again in Latium: Simois and Xanthus are to be recognized in the Latian Tiber and Numicus and on the plains between them is to be played out the coming struggle.

After tracing the lines of his camp on the bank of the river, Aeneas then chooses out a hundred envoys and sends them to the king's palace, bearing gifts, and craving a peaceful welcome for the Trojans.[3] After traversing the way (perhaps the words 'iter emensi' suggest some considerable distance) they can see the towers and roofs of the Latins, and they then approach the wall and the level exercising grounds. The king summons them to his presence, where he sits on his ancestral throne beneath the high roof and hundred lofty columns of his palace, which stands on the city's crown. Its surroundings are woods full of superstitious dread, and revered for ancient worship observed from the days of his ancestors.

> *Tectum augustum, ingens, centum sublime columnis*
> *urbe fuit summa, Laurentis regia Pici,*
> *horrendum silvis et religione parentum.*[4]

Here in the temple-palace, which was also the king's council house, Latinus received them, where ancient images of bygone kings looked down upon them from the walls or stood upon the threshold: Italus, Sabinus, and Janus, all the storied line of Laurentian kings. Spoils of war adorned the door-posts, beaks of ships, and an image of Picus, tamer of horses, who was changed into a bird with coloured wings, the woodpecker, by his lovelorn wife the enchantress, Circe. So the Trojans enter into the presence of Latinus, and he receives them amid the splendours and traditional memorials of his ancient house. Such is Vergil's conception, picked out with epic grandeur and exaggeration, of the city and the palace standing on its *arx*, a place full of old tradition, royally established under the rule of a noble king.

[1] See above, p. 69 sq. [2] *Aen.*, VI, 86-9. [3] *Ibid.*, VII, 152-91.
[4] *Ibid.*, VII, 170-2.

The reply of Ilioneus, the herald, to Latinus' questions contains significant words. After explaining their arrival in his land, he tells how they have come at the bidding of Apollo:

> *huc repetit iussisque ingentibus urguet Apollo*
> *Tyrrhenum ad Thybrim et fontis vada sacra Numici.*[1]

The Tiber is once again mentioned in close connection with the Numicus just as in the lines already quoted which describe the reconnaissances of the Trojans. In the latter place it has been seen that the Numicus marks the limit of their exploring, but what is the implication of this second reference? This cannot be a meaningless repetition of the earlier lines, for Ilioneus has reached the peroration of his appeal for a peaceful welcome. From their vantage ground on the Tiber's bank, the heralds had gone forth as far as the Numicus, that is to the city of Latinus, as had the scouts before them. The scouts had reconnoitred the city. Plainly the city and the river have a close connection; otherwise the reference to the river is at this point irrelevant.

Later in the *Aeneid* another indication of the nature of the site is given. After the long and indecisive struggle between the Latin tribes and the Trojans and their allies, Latinus in council tries to suggest terms of peace, offering to furnish supplies for them to build ships even as many as twenty of Italian oak, or more should they wish, so that they may leave Latium.[2] 'All the timber lies at the water's edge . . . let all provide them with bronze tackle, workmen . . . and dockyard.' The high significance of these words cannot be denied. Since Latinus can offer all that could be needed for building ships, including the very dockyards, Laurentum must have a connection with, or access to, the sea. The shore must be safe for ships, and have good harbourage, if such a proposal can be made in all sincerity. The oak trees of the maritime forest[3] were there on the fringe of the shore as they still are at many places along the Latian coast from Ostia to Antium. It is then most appropriate that there should be timber for shipbuilding near Laurentum if the city has a relation to the Latian shore.

Yet more important evidence for topography is to be gathered from the closing scenes of the *Aeneid*. The arena is

[1] *Aen.*, VII, 241-2.   [2] *Ibid.*, XI, 327-9.
[3] See above, Introduction, p. xii.

PLATE 34. Sulphur lake at Albunea showing bubbling springs (see page 108)

PLATE 35. Interior of the 'Grotto of Albunea' (see page 108)

PLATE 36.   Dragoncello, ancient Ficana (see page 113)

prepared for the contest between Aeneas and Turnus beneath the walls of the city:

> campum ad certamen magnae sub moenibus urbis
> dimensi Rutulique viri Teucrique parabant.[1]

There due sacrifice is made by both sides. After the oaths have been taken by Aeneas and Turnus, a change comes over the hearts of the Rutuli, and they are incited to join in a general fight by the intervention of Juturna, especially through the omen which she sends. An eagle disturbs a shore bird, and, when pursued, it drops its prey into the river.

> namque volans rubra fulvus Iovis ales in aethra
> litoreas agitabat avis turbamque sonantem
> agminis aligeri, subito cum lapsus ad undas
> cycnum excellentem pedibus rapit improbus uncis.
> arrexere animos Itali, cunctaeque volucres
> convertunt clamore fugam (mirabile visu),
> aetheraque obscurant pennis hostemque per auras
> facta nube premunt, donec vi victus et ipso
> pondere defecit praedamque ex unguibus ales
> proiecit fluvio, penitusque in nubila fugit.[2]

There is no contradiction in the use of the words *litoreas* and *fluvio*. These were birds which frequented the waters near the river's mouth. Even at the present day the lagoons near the Laurentian shore are the haunt of great flocks of birds which hover over the waters, often rising as one body and again swooping down in search of food. That the birds in the omen should be called shore birds presents no difficulty in interpretation, neither does the statement that the eagle dropped his prey into the river, since river and shore are so close together.[3]

Then follows the general uproar when both the watching ranks engage in fight, until Aeneas is induced by his mother to make an attack upon the city itself, for its walls tower over the scene as he seeks out Turnus in the fray, and their very quietness and safety incite him to a greater venture:

> huc atque huc acies circumtulit, aspicit urbem
> immunem tanti belli atque impune quietam.[4]

[1] *Aen.*, XII, 116-17.   [2] *Ibid.*, XII, 247-56.
[3] Cf. *Aen.*, XII, 261-3:
> o miseri, quos improbus advena bello
> territat, invalidas ut avis, et litora vestra
> vi populat.
[4] *Aen.*, XII, 558-9.

H

Through all the events of the twelfth book we never seem to lose sight of the walls of Laurentum; the spectators look down from the battlements upon the struggle, and the walls are even attacked with the battering-ram.[1]

Then comes the culminating and closing event of the whole *Aeneid*, the heroic single combat between Trojan Aeneas and Laurentian Turnus, explicitly for the hand of Lavinia, but in reality for the whole glory and justification of Rome's greatness. In the first encounter Turnus' spear is shattered to pieces against the divine armour of Aeneas. Here comes what is perhaps the clearest indication of all of the site of Laurentum as Vergil conceived it. When Turnus finds himself unarmed, he turns to flee, but his flight is checked, for he is hemmed in on all sides by the Trojan onlookers, and, what is more and indeed of high significance, *a great marsh*, and the *high city walls*. These lines, added to what has preceded, are a clear indication of the site of Laurentum. The detail of the *palus* is no epic conceit, but a clear statement of topography.

> *undique enim densa Teucri inclusere corona*
> *atque hinc vasta palus, hinc ardua moenia cingunt.*[2]

The field of combat lies between the two, since he is so completely cut off from flight. The river is near, as has been shown, and so is the shore.

Lastly, in the course of the combat, Aeneas' spear becomes lodged in the stump of a wild olive tree, an old tree connected with the lore of that place, sacred to the Laurentian god, Faunus; it is a tree on which in olden times sailors had been used to hang up their garments as votive offerings to the god.

> *Forte sacer Fauno foliis oleaster amaris*
> *hic steterat, nautis olim venerabile lignum,*
> *servati ex undis ubi figere dona solebant*
> *Laurenti divo et votas suspendere vestis.*[3]

As well as an interesting piece of forgotten folk-lore, again there is a reference to the sea. Sailors came home to Laurentum. That is a clear indication of her communication with the sea and of the old tradition of a landing-beach on the Laurentian shore.[4]

This then is the Laurentum of Vergil. His topography

---

[1] *Aen.*, XII, 704-7.   [2] *Ibid.*, XII, 744-5.   [3] *Ibid.*, XII, 767-70.
[4] See above, pp. 1 sq., and 89 sq.

suggests a city crowned with a king's palace which contains memorials of his ancient destiny and proud traditions, named after an ancient laurel revered for its sanctity. It stands on a river, beside a plain, and near a great marsh. Not once, but several times is the sea mentioned. Aeneas may build ships for his safe departure; the shore birds are disturbed by the eagle; and it is sailors who hung up votive offerings to Faunus. Laurentum is indeed a city whose business is with the sea. It has been said that Vergil's topography is never clear; yet this investigation has shown that there are many hints, sometimes clear indications, both sometimes veiled in poetic style, of the site of Laurentum as he conceived it.

The river, beside the banks of which the final scenes of combat are played out, is left nameless, but the description of the city's site beside a great marsh can leave little doubt that it is the Numicus, and that for Vergil Laurentum lay near the *stagna*, and not far from the sea. It might, however, be argued that the distance of the Numicus from the Tiber, some sixteen miles, is against such a location. A study of the movements of the tenth and eleventh books will throw light on the question. In the tenth, Turnus is transported, against his will, from the midst of the battle, and taken by sea to Ardea.

> *labitur alta secans fluctuque aestuque secundo*
> *et patris antiquam Dauni defertur ad urbem.*[1]

Not the slightest doubt can be entertained about the topography of this incident, for Turnus is taken full twenty miles away. A preparation is thus made for the shifting of the scene from the bank of the Tiber to bring in the second river of the Sibyl's prophecy.[2] By a masterly stroke of dramatic artistry, one of the two chief protagonists is removed to the farther limit of the Latian stage. He is next found sitting in the council of war at Laurentum. There is nothing to prevent the Trojan advance from the Tiber covering some sixteen miles; in fact, the distance enhances the excitement of their coming. They are said to be proceeding over all the plain when the news is brought:

> *instructos acie Tiberino a flumine Teucros*
> *Tyrrhenamque manum totis descendere campis.*[3]

---

[1] *Aen.*, X, 687-8.   [2] *Ibid.*, VI, 86-9; see above, p. 95.
[3] *Ibid.*, XI, 449-50.

The open ground for unimpeded advance was to be found above the marshy forested coastline. Aeneas comes by the mountain range:

ipse ardua montis
per deserta iugo superans adventat ad urbem.[1]

This is the higher ground, the last seaward ridge of the Alban *massif* which crosses the Campagna and on which stand Ardea and Lavinium. Carcopino[2] claims to have found the valley where Turnus[3] sets his ambush, lying in wait for Aeneas near Lavinium, and makes this a strong point in his identification of the site with Laurentum. Suffice it to say that such a sunken valley as this with an unexpected plateau above, is characteristic of the whole Campagna, and many such could be found between the Tiber and the Numicus.

If this interpretation of Vergil's Laurentum be right, it is deeply significant for the worship of *Pater Indiges* which had a part in the Roman state cults of Latium. We know that the deified Aeneas was worshipped under this title at a temple in a grove by the Numicus, and that the consuls and *pontifices* used to make annual sacrifice there.[4] The cult of this god must have been as well known and familiar as that of the *Penates* at Lavinium, and those observed at Ardea. It may be that at the rites of the *Indiges*, who was thought to be the indwelling spirit of the Numicus, the tales of the Aeneas-legend were told just as Strabo informs us they were told at the federal cult festivals at Ardea.[5] Ovid[6] beautifies the legend by telling how Venus washed away Aeneas' mortality in the river, and made him a god. Aeneas, idealized, is brought by Vergil to the Numicus stream to play out, not the mortal combat which should translate him to heaven, but a conflict which should prove him victor in the struggle for the future existence of Rome.

The ancient records show that on the Laurentian shore were ruins which had become incorporated in the Aeneas-legends:[7]

[1] *Aen.*, XI, 513-14.
[2] Carcopino, *V.O.O.*, 1919, p. 333 sq.
[3] *Aen.*, XI, 526-31.
[4] See above, p. 78 sq. Pliny, *N.H.*, III, 56; Sil It., VIII, 39; Dion. Hal., *A.R.*, I, 64; Schol. Ver., *Ad Aen.*, I, 260; Arnobius, *Ad Nationes*, I, 36; Servius, *Ad Aen.*, IV, 620.
[5] Strabo, V, 232, and p. 45 sq. above.
[6] Ovid, *Met.*, XIV, 607 sq.
[7] See above, p. 87 sq.

near the *stagna* and the sea probably stood the temple of *Pater Indiges*, the *heroon* known to Dionysius.[1] The high ground of Campo Iemini,[2] where the tufa ridge of the Alban *massif*, on which are situated both Ardea and Lavinium, comes within two kilometres of the shore, standing as it does on a dominant position by the river Numicus and commanding its lower valley and the seaward plain, is not unsuitable for a cult site. This perhaps was the scene of the rites of the *Indiges*, and that envisaged by the poet as the setting for the closing events of the epic. This inquiry must be left, in the present state of knowledge, in the region of conjecture, but perhaps it is not too fanciful to surmise that Vergil may have visited this place, and, seeing its ancient memorials, may have thought, as did his contemporaries, that traces of an ancient city were here, as at Ardea and Lavinium.

EXCURSUS ON PLINY'S NOTICE OF LAURENTUM

Pliny[3] writes in his *Natural History*: 'in principio est Ostia colonia . . . oppidum Laurentum, lucus Iovis Indigetis, amnis Numicius, Ardea'. The direction followed is from north to south, as is shown by the mention of the Numicus before Ardea. This alone is certain, for the rest of the passage will bear several interpretations, each equally doubtful. It is impossible in the first place to decide whether *Laurentum* is the name of the town, or a genitive plural of *Laurentes*.

1 The reference may be to the lost early settlement,[4] but if that be so, there is nothing in the rest of the passage to help in locating it, especially since there is no mention of Lavinium.

2 If it be taken to mean Lavinium, this form of nomenclature seems remarkable, especially since both the site of Lavinium and the name were not lost in Roman times.

[1] Dion. Hal., *A.R.*, I, 64. A temple is mentioned by the Schol. Ver. and by Ovid as quoted in the preceding page, notes 4 and 6.
[2] Roman remains are to be seen in the courtyard of the farmhouse, but appear to have belonged to a villa.
[3] Pliny, *N.H.*, III, 56.
[4] See above, p. 83 sq.

3 A recent theory of Bendz[1] would identify the *lucus* with
Lavinium and refer Laurentum to a supposed site in the
neighbourhood of Capocotta. The only foundation for
this is that the modern name of Pratica is thought to be
derived from *Pater Indiges*. This seems unsound reasoning,
for the name has not been traced back to Roman times.
The various accounts[2] of the legendary battle on the
banks of the Numicus near the *stagna*, during which
Aeneas was drowned, or miraculously disappeared, in the
river, to be thereafter deified and worshipped as *Pater
Indiges*, show clearly that the grove was beside the river,
so that Bendz's theory is thus proved untenable.

4 Ten kilometres south of the Tiber, dating from Augustan
times, there existed in Pliny's time the Vicus Augustanus
Laurentum. The name is authenticated by many inscriptions found during the excavations.[3] This may be the
only Laurentum known to Pliny and the style *oppidum*
would well suit it.

---

[1] Bendz, *Opuscula Archaeologica*, I[1], 1934, p. 62 sq.   [2] See above, p. 73.
[3] *C.I.L.*, XIV, 2040 sq., and above, p. 84.

CHAPTER VI

ALBUNEA[1]

At rex sollicitus monstris oracula Fauni,
fatidici genitoris, adit lucosque sub alta
consulit Albunea, nemorum quae maxima sacro
fonte sonat saevamque exhalat opaca mephitim.
hinc Italae gentes omnisque Oenotria tellus
in dubiis responsa petunt.[2]

AT the time when Aeneas, destined by Fate to be the husband of Lavinia, reached the Tiber, portents[3] which forboded ill took place in the king's palace at Laurentum. Then it was that King Latinus, troubled at these portents, consulted the oracle sacred to his prophetic father Faunus. He went to the groves in deep-wooded Albunea, where foul sulphurous fumes came forth from the depths of the earth, and where strange sounds could be heard. This oracle was widely known, and many of the Italian races came here to seek an answer to their perplexities. The custom was for the suppliant, acting himself as priest, to bring hither his gifts, and then to lie down to sleep on the skins of the victims of sacrifice. He would see flitting shapes in many a strange appearance, and hear voices, converse with the gods, and speak to Acheron in the depths of Avernus:

huc dona sacerdos
cum tulit et caesarum ovium sub nocte silenti
pellibus incubuit stratis somnosque petivit,
multa modis simulacra videt volitantia miris,
et varias audit voces fruiturque deorum
colloquio atque imis Acheronta adfatur Avernis.[4]

As Latinus slept, a voice from the grove spoke, warning him that the gods forbade Lavinia's betrothal to Turnus, and that a foreign husband was to be hers. When the Trojan envoys came to have audience with Latinus he recognized in the coming of them and their leader, direct fulfilment of the oracle's words.[5]

[1] The substance of this chapter was published in *J.R.S.*, 1934, pp. 25-30, and is here reproduced by kind permission of the Council of the Society for the Promotion of Roman Studies.
[2] *Aen.*, VII, 81-6.   [3] *Ibid.*, VII, 64-80.   [4] *Ibid.*, VII, 86-91.
[5] *Ibid.*, VII, 259-73.

The traditional view from the time of Servius onwards has been that the oracle was situated in the neighbourhood of Tibur, and that the waters described are those of the sulphur lakes of Albula, white and strong-smelling, which lie two miles away from Tivoli (ancient Tibur) in the tract of open country beneath the Sabine hills; to quote Servius' words: 'alta, quia est in Tiburtinis altissimis montibus. et Albunea dicta est ab aquae qualitate, quae in illo fonte est . . . sciendum sane unum nomen fuisse fontis et silvae'.[1] These springs, now called Aque Albule, are on the road to Tivoli from Rome at the place called Bagni, where is a flat plain covered by white deposits from the springs which well up from the ground. The water is bluish-white, and is strongly impregnated with sulphur and carbonate of lime.[2] On the west bank are considerable remains of an ancient bath which show that the water and its properties were prized in Roman times. That these Tiburtine springs were called Albula in Roman times cannot be doubted, from the inscriptions unearthed in these very baths,[3] and the name is also recorded by Vitruvius when he writes of sulphur springs: 'sunt . . . fontes . . . qui . . . perveniunt supra terram sapore odore coloreque corrupto ut in Tiburtina via flumen Albula'.[4]

The view that the Albunea of Vergil was to be located near Tibur was first challenged by Bonstetten[5] in 1805, and his theory has been further developed by Carcopino.[6] The main objections to the old view are, firstly, that Albula lies about thirty miles north, in the Sabine region, well away both from the district in which is set the action of the last six books of the *Aeneid*, and from the home of Latinus, which, as has been seen, was most probably at Laurentum, near the mouth of the Numicus; secondly, from the difference in name, since that of Albula is so well attested by ancient notices; and thirdly from the difficulty of access. Both Bonstetten and Carcopino are in

---

[1] Servius, *Ad Aen.*, VII, 83.
[2] Ashby, *The Roman Campagna in Classical Times*, 1927, p. 99.
[3] Ashby, *ibid.*, *C.I.L.*, XIV, 3908 sq.
[4] Vitr., VIII, 3. Also Mart., *Ep.*, 1, 12; Statius, 1, 3, 74. The name *Albunea* that occurs in Horace, *Odes*, 1, 7, 12, has been a stumbling-block to scholars since it obviously refers to the locality of Tibur. It is, however, only the name of the nymph of the white cascades of the Anio; see G. F. Hallam, *Horace at Tibur and the Sabine Farm*, 2nd ed., p. 30.
[5] Bonstetten, *Voyage dans Le Latium*, 1861², pp. 204-15.
[6] Carcopino, *V.O.O.*, 1919, pp. 338-44.

agreement in locating the oracle at the sulphur springs near
Pratica di Mare, ancient Lavinium; neither, however, investigated the site as fully as was desirable, and herein are given
the results of a further exploration.

From Pratica there is a road leading by way of Pavona to
Albano, probably on the line of a very ancient route[1] that may
have connected Lavinium with Alba Longa. After about three
hours' walk from Pratica this road is crossed by the so-called
Via Laurentina which leads from Rome to Ardea. Near the
crossing, and on the east of the latter road, a sulphurous region
extends for nearly a mile in the direction of Albano, and is
known now by the name of Zolforata[2] (pl. 30.) Just before
the cross-roads are reached a strong sulphurous smell begins
to be noticeable, proceeding from a narrow valley which, after
a few hundred yards, opens out into a wide, shallow, crater-like
formation in area a quarter to half a square mile, and surrounded by low undulating hills scarred here and there by
outcrops of whitish-yellow rocks. The level green pasture is
pocked with round barren patches where all growth has been
prevented by the effusion of a sulphur spring which, if not
active at the moment, has left a thin deposit, giving an impression of a white sprinkling on the brown earth. When seen
in October 1933, some of these shallow depressions were quite
dry, but others were filled with milky-white sulphurous water
that welled up through many small holes in the ground, accompanied by a sizzling and bubbling sound; rain water, however,
often collects in them so that they become shallow pools. The
temperature of the water[3] is 15 degrees Centigrade (59 degrees
Fahrenheit), although Nibby[4] describes it as hot, perhaps because he had not examined the place in detail. Nothing more
uncanny than this seething cloudy water and strong-smelling
vapour could be wished, and to the ancients all this region
must have been highly 'religiosus'; for here were outlets from
the nether world filled with strange sights and sounds. In all
probability in Roman times, the whole of this sulphurous
region was densely covered with primeval forest left intact
because of the superstition attached both to springs of this kind

[1] Ashby, *The Roman Campagna in Classical Times*, 1927, p. 209.
[2] There are various forms of this name, Solforata, Solfatara, Solfarata, but the most usual is Zolforata.
[3] Perrone, *Carta idrografica d'Italia*, no.º 26 bis Tevere², 1908, p. 233.
[4] Nibby, *Analisi della Carta dei Dintorni di Roma*, vol. III, 1848², p. 103.

and to sacred groves.[1] To the north-east on the top of a low but steep hill is Tor Tignosa, a ruined mediaeval tower which adds its contribution to the desolation of the place.

The valley becomes narrower at this point, and after skirting the base of the hill one reaches a short lateral valley where there are more discharges of sulphur causing a large expanse of barren soil. When seen after heavy rain in January, this was covered with water, forming a large shallow pool. In the hillside, which is steep, but could not be described as high, and is covered with small woodland trees, are three small caves which, from their regular shapes and sharp angles may be recognized as artificial (pl. 31). The cave on the left contains a sulphur spring, and the middle one a fresh water spring much frequented by the shepherds. To the left of these caves and a little higher up the hillside is a small crater-like formation, and on one side of it a perpendicular rock-face pierced by an artificial cave that has a short lateral gallery at the end. In early November, before the winter rains, the crater was quite dry, but in the gallery of the cave there was water, which was quite still, although the bubbling sound of a subterranean sulphur spring could be heard. In early January, after the rains, the crater had become a small lake, and the cave was filled with water to within two-and-a-half feet of the roof, so as to be quite impenetrable. Pl. 32 shows the crater in this condition.

This is apparently the place recognized by Bonstetten as the site of the oracle. His account, full of the delight of first impressions and the enthusiasm of locating a Vergilian site, is most vivid: 'Tout à coup j'aperçois un petit étang d'une eau laiteuse d'où s'échappaient de grosses bulles d'air, et dont on faisait fortement bouillonner l'eau en la remuant. Le terrain tout alentour était blanc et le bassin se trouvait placé sous un rocher volcanique tout blanc, presque à pic, assez élevé, où l'on voyait à travers des herbes les traces de plusieurs cascades qui devaient tomber dans le bassin pardessus l'entrée d'une caverne faite de main d'homme à ce qu'il me semblait. Elle avait quatre à cinq pieds de haut, environ quinze de profondeur, sur six à sept de large. Je la trouvai pleine de cette même eau bouillonante, dont les pétillements fréquents et le siffle-

[1] Frazer, *Magic Art*, II, 1911, pp. 121-3; several examples are given in this passage, and another in Ovid, *Fasti*, IV, 649.

ment léger produisaient dans cette voûte mille bruits bizarres. Qu'on se représente ... ces arbres touffus, ce profond silence, cette obscurité mystérieuse, cette odeur de soufre concentrée dans l'épaisseur de l'ombrage, et ces roches éclatantes ... A tous ces traits je crus reconnaître l'Albunea de Virgile.'[1] Thus was Bonstetten the first among the moderns to recognize the true locality of the oracle of Faunus, although on the other hand he was rather hasty in assuming that this cavern marked the actual spot; for he admits that it looks artificial, and probably he did not know to what extent it could be flooded after rain. Further, from his account it is clear that he did not survey the whole region thoroughly, but, led by his guide along the top of the hillside to the crater, he recognized this, the first possible place he saw, as the site. He is followed by Nibby,[2] and also by Carcopino, who locates here what he styles 'the Grotto of Albunea', after having gone over the ground in 1912. It is to be noted that Bonstetten mentions only this one cave, and it seems impossible for him not to have seen any of the other three if they then existed. Perrone refers only to the two which contain springs. Carcopino quotes Perrone's statement mentioning no other caves. Thus it may be deduced that all the four caves are of recent excavation.

The modern name 'Zolforata', which can be traced back to the thirteenth century,[3] is significant; for it is the Italian for a sulphur mine. Perrone in 1908, speaking of the two caves containing sulphur springs, says that they were cut into the hillside to extract sulphur, but have been disused for many years. Nibby, writing in 1837, speaks as if in his day sulphur were actually mined in the crater: 'una specie di cratere dove si cava il solfo'.[4] What is more, from the regular shape of the crater, the looseness of the surrounding earth, and the flatness of the rock-face, it may reasonably be inferred that the whole is artificial, and was dug out in mining operations to make the rock accessible. Thus both Bonstetten and Carcopino located the oracle in what is probably a disused modern sulphur mine.

Neither of these two scholars seems to have explored farther than this point. About two hundred yards farther up the main valley is a large barren expanse, which in October was a waste

[1] Bonstetten, *Voyage dans le Latium*, 1861², pp. 205-6.
[2] Nibby, *Analisi della Carta dei Dintorni di Roma*, vol. III, 1848², pp. 100-3.
[3] Nibby, *ibid.*, p. 100.   [4] Nibby, *ibid.*, p. 101.

of half-dried mud with a small funnel-shaped hole at one point through which could be heard subterranean boiling and seething sounds. In early January this had become a small lake (pl. 34), full of milky-white water, troubled and resonant with sulphur springs. This lake, or possibly the one in the crater described above, both of which are only filled with water after the winter rains, may be that mentioned by both Nibby and Tomassetti[1] as having been marked in Ameti's map and having since disappeared.[2]

Crossing the valley, and skirting the farther end of the lake, there runs an ancient road, as is proved by a few Roman paving-stones lying on the grass, and an artificial cutting in the hillside to the north; the line of it can just be discerned in (pl. 34) in the background, to the left under the hillside. It is part of the ancient Via Ardeatina that ran from Rome to Ardea, and its presence there helps to prove that these springs must have been well known in antiquity.[3]

Less than a quarter of a mile farther up the main valley, the floor of which is scarred by some half-dozen small round sulphur beds, under the hillside, there is a large cave that shows no signs of artificiality (pl. 33). It is roughly nine feet high, fifteen wide, and twenty deep. Within is a copious sulphur spring (pl. 35), which bubbles loudly and hisses like a great cauldron. Reflected by the roof of the cave, which acts as a natural sounding-board, the noise can be heard plainly at a distance of nearly a hundred yards. The overflow trickles from the entrance making all the ground in front of it barren. This natural cave, with its weird sounds and mysteriously troubled waters, is by far the most remarkable feature of the region, but strangely enough, it is not mentioned by any investigator of the Campagna whom the writer has been able to consult.[4] This cave cannot be that chosen by Bonstetten and Carcopino, for the dimensions are substantially greater; there

---

[1] Tomassetti, *La Campagna Romana*, II, 1910, p. 439.

[2] A small lake is marked in the following early maps: Eufrosino della Volpaia, 1547; Antonio Vallardi, 1766; Müller, *Roms Campagna*, 1824.

[3] Dr. Axel Boëthius, Director of the Swedish Archaeological Institute at Rome, is the authority for this statement. The modern so-called Via Laurentina that leads from Rome to Ardea follows the ancient Ardeatina for several kilometres at the beginning and end of its course.

[4] These include Nibby, *Analisi della Carta dei Dintorni di Roma*, 1837 and 1848; Tomassetti, *La Campagna Romana*, 1910; Ashby, *The Roman Campagna in Classical Times*, 1929.

is nowhere in it any appearance of artificiality, and there is no crater near it.

The Romans may well have called all this region 'Albunea', a name derived from the white appearance of the sulphur deposits which must have included both the springs and the woods, and is coupled by Vergil with 'alta'. There is no hill anywhere near that could possibly be termed high, not even relatively when one stands at the foot of those with which the valley is girt, and not even by poetical exaggeration, for the Alban Mount dominates all the scene, and so to designate what are mere hummocks in comparison would be scarcely conceivable (pl. 30). 'Alta' then may either refer to the height of the trees or else mean 'deep', being used to describe the denseness of the forest and the seclusion of the valley. It follows that 'sub' implies not 'at the foot of a hill', as it has usually been understood, but 'within the forest'.[1]

The question next arises about the significance of 'lucos'. Servius tells us that, wherever Vergil uses the word, it has a religious connection.[2] The derivation is from 'luceo' and therefore the root meaning is 'an open place in a wood'.[3] As has already been said, wherever there is an outcrop of sulphur, vegetation cannot grow, and round barren patches of soil, sometimes covered with water, appear in the grass: neither could there have been trees where the deadly sulphur spread in the woods of Albunea, and the clearings so caused are probably the 'luci' of which Vergil speaks. Each one of them would undoubtedly be regarded with 'religio', a feeling of superstitious fear; for here were outlets from the nether world through which emerged deadly vapours and awesome sounds. The words

> nemorum quae maxima sacro
> fonte sonat

have always caused perplexity, but they become clear when considered in relation to the topography of Zolforata. 'Sonat' is used to describe the sound of a bubbling sulphur spring, and not that of a cascade as has been thought by those who would put the oracle near Tibur. The sound varies in strength in different places, but it is the clearest and loudest when heard

---

[1] Cf. *Aen.*, VIII, 125, where the phrase *subeunt luco* appears.
[2] *Ad Aen.*, I, 310.   [3] Cf. Livy, XXIV, 3, 4.

echoing in a cave. The word 'sacer' as often, here means more than merely 'sacred', but something uncanny, dangerous, and inexplicable,[1] something from which man might shrink in fear; 'execrabilis', as Servius says, commenting on 'sacrum Argiletum'.[2] Thus it is seen how Vergil's phraseology is in every particular in accord with the appearance of the region called Zolforata, and that the passage quoted at the head of this chapter may be translated thus:

> 'But the king, alarmed by the portents, goes to the oracle of Faunus, his prophetic father, and consults the groves within deep-wooded Albunea, forest without peer, which murmurs with its awesome spring, and gives forth in the shade foul vapour. Hence the folk of Italy and the whole Oenotrian land seek answers in their doubts.'

In the ancient commentary on Vergil, which was formerly assigned to Probus, the oracle is unhesitatingly placed in the above locality: 'itaque etiam oraculum eius [Fauni] in Albunea Laurentinorum silva est'.[3] The date of the author is uncertain, but he probably wrote not later than the second century A.D., whereas Servius belongs to the fourth. Perhaps it is to be deduced that the oracle was forgotten during the later times of the Empire, especially since Faunus never became a civilized god, and never had an organized cult in the city, but always remained a *numen* of the woodland and pasture,[4] in one of his aspects gifted with prophetic powers. The difference between the direct statement quoted and the confusion shown by Servius may perhaps bear out this theory. That the oracle is to be located at Zolforata is highly probable, and in that district by far the most likely site as it now exists is the cave shown in pls. 33 and 35, which is natural and filled with the sound of sulphurous waters. On the other hand, unfortunately, it cannot be assumed that the spring was there two thousand years ago, and the final deduction, therefore, is that the oracle was somewhere in the place now called Zolforata, but that the exact location must always remain a matter of doubt.

[1] Warde Fowler in *J.R.S.*, I, 1911, p. 57, on 'The Original Meaning of the Word "*sacer*".'
[2] Servius, *Ad Aen.*, VIII, 345.
[3] Probus, *Ad Georg.*, I, 10.
[4] Warde Fowler, *Roman Festivals of the Republic*, 1899, pp. 257-63; and especially pp. 262-3, where Ovid's account of a woodland oracle of Faunus is mentioned: *Fasti*, III, 291 sq.

This oracle, tended by no priest but only by the suppliant himself, set in the midst of strange natural phenomena, not far from the ancient Via Ardeatina from which wayfarers might turn to consult the god, an awesome place through which the superstitious traveller might pass in haste with his mantle close about him, under the tutelage of Faunus, the god of the wild woodland and of the flocks and herds, may have been the scene of one of the most primitive cults of the Roman Campagna. There is no sign of any monuments connected with it, and it is to be considered a natural shrine untouched by the hand of man. Perhaps the shepherds of old time came here to learn their fortunes from their own presiding deity, and made sacrifice to him of the sheep of their own rearing.

The details of the rites as given by Vergil sound genuine enough, though it is for others to decide whether the poet has given the procedure a Greek dress, since some authorities consider that the custom of incubation is essentially Greek. Well might such a place become the site of a rustic oracle. Here were vapours bubbling up from under the earth, to Roman belief, veritably from Avernus itself: well might the believing peasant have thought that here were indeed outlets from the nether world. Well might a man, sleeping alone by the weird springs in the darkness, have translated the sound of their welling-up into mingled voices, in the stillness of the primeval forest grown louder, until he thought that the gods themselves spoke to him: well might he too imagine strange forms that flitted about him in his dreams, and revealed to him the future.

We have in Vergil's account of this rustic oracle yet another example of his predilection for the humble yet sacred places of the countryside which he loved so well. In taking Latinus to consult it, in heroic wise he is but seeing a local shepherd make consultation at his own oracle, the primitive shrine revered by the Italian races; the awesome spot known to wayfarers, and surely to the poet himself, curious of all things pertaining to the countryman's creed.

CHAPTER VII

FICANA AND THE AGER SOLONIUS IN THE *AENEID*

> est antiquus ager Tusco mihi proximus amni,
> longus in occasum fines, super usque Sicanos;
> Aurunci Rutulique serunt, et vomere duros
> exercent collis atque horum asperrima pascunt.
> haec omnis regio et celsi plaga pinea montis
> cedat amicitiae Teucrorum.[1]

WITH these words Latinus suggests to a meeting of the chiefs of the Latins, a condition on which peace, and indeed a lasting peace, might be made with Aeneas. He is willing to cede part of his own territory, an ancient land, stretching towards the sunset, bordering on that of the Sicani, and adjacent to the Tiber, tilled by the Aurunci and the men of Ardea. The question to be decided is whether Vergil had in mind a particular place of historic and antiquarian interest to be recognized in these lines.

Along the Tiber's bank there is an eminence overhanging the water about four miles above Ostia where ends, by the river, the last ridge of the Alban *massif* and the last high land before the sea is reached, and the only high land by the river for several miles either way. A study of the geology of the Tiber's course has shown that the salt marsh below this particular place is all the result of the silting up of alluvial deposit brought down from the soft volcanic rock through which the river flows, and is, therefore, of comparatively recent origin.[2] The rate of this process is easily calculated when it is realized that Ostia, once the port of Rome, is now three miles away from the sea. In prehistoric, or early historic times, the Tiber's mouth must have been at a spot much higher up even than Ostia, much nearer, in fact, this very cliff-like eminence (see fig. 36) than in Vergil's time. This must have been a highly strategic site, and it is here that archaeologists would locate the ancient city of Ficana which was a forerunner of Ostia in very

---

[1] *Aen.*, XI, 316-21.
[2] Carcopino, *V.O.O.*, p. 501, and above, p. 4 sq.

early Roman history.[1] Festus records that Ficana was situated at the eleventh milestone on the Via Ostiensis, upon certain rocks called Puilia.[2] This must have been a very important place in those far-off times, for not only was it the small port near the river's mouth, but it probably also faced an early Etruscan port near Galera on the other side. The name is also vouched for in Pliny's list of extinct cities of Latium.[3] In the time of the kings the city was captured by Ancus Martius,[4] so tradition says, and its inhabitants transported to Rome, and settled on the Aventine hill. This may have happened when this same king[5] started the salt workings near the site of Ostia, and so this tradition is really only a reflection of the seaward advance of early Rome.[6]

The site of Ficana, now called Dragoncello, a small estate situated on Monte Cugno between the Tiber and the confluence of Malafede, can be reached by taking a path through the fields from the modern Via Ostiensis, or on the other side of the river from Ponte Galera, where there is a station on the line to Fiumicino, about two miles away. The cliff is now crowned by a farmhouse and at the foot the river can be ferried in a small boat, perhaps as it always has been (pl. 36). In the ploughed fields near, the writer found many a sherd and broken brick of the times of the Empire, and saw fixed into the wall of the house a poor specimen of late Roman sculpture. In the river bank a casual find was made of a piece of black glazed Campanian ware of about the second century B.C. Until systematic excavation has been carried out, however, all that can be said for certain is that the site was inhabited in late Roman times, and was most probably occupied by a villa.

Carcopino[7] would see in the lines from the *Aeneid* quoted above a reference to the ancient city of Ficana, holding, as it once did, a commanding position overlooking the river. He would hold that the name Sicani is the latinized form of the

---

[1] Ashby, *J.R.S.*, 1912, p. 153, suggests that the existence of the cult of *Mars Ficanus* at Ostia (*C.I.L.*, XIV, 309) implies that Ostia was heir to Ficana.

[2] Festus, *sub voce* 'Puilia': *Puilia saxa esse ad portum qui sit secundum Tiberi, ait Fabius Pictor . . . ubi fuerit Ficana via Ostiensi ad lapidem undecimum.*

[3] Pliny, *N.H.*, III, 56.

[4] Dion. Hal., *A.R.*, III, 38; Livy, I, XIII.

[5] The traditional founding of Ostia is discredited by archaeological finds, but the salt marshes were probably worked in the time of the kings. See above, p. 13 sq.

[6] Last, *C.A.H.*, vol. VII, 378.

[7] *V.O.O.*, 1919, 458-68.

Σύκανοι, derived from σύκος, and that since *f* and *s* are often interchangeable in transliteration from the Greek, Sicani can be considered equivalent to Ficani, and Sicana to Ficana. Whether Carcopino be right or wrong in recognizing in these lines a reference to the old pre-Ostian city on the Tiber's bank, there would seem to be reason for accepting the suggestion when regard is made to the poet's love of antique tradition and ancient places.

Inquiry may proceed further to discover what is the *ager* of which Latinus speaks. It cannot evidently be Ficana itself, for he says that the tract of land extends to, and touches upon, its boundaries. Those who till the soil are not the Sicani or the Ficani, but the Aurunci and the Rutuli. We can, however, with certainty, accept Carcopino's explanation of the words 'longus in occasum' as implying the direction towards Ostia: indeed Servius' commentary has the words: 'potuit ergo usque ad Laurentum et ad Hostiam tendi';[1] showing that to the author it was explicable as a piece of land stretching westward towards the old port of Rome.

In Roman times a piece of land extending from the Tiber to the Volscian and Campanian frontiers was known as the Ager Solonius; it was historic, coming early into the possession of the Romans, and its borders were ancient; but little, unfortunately, is now known of it. We may judge from Roman writers, however, something of its topography. A notice of Festus[2] indicating the site of an old city called Pomonal gives evidence of the western extension of the ager: 'Pomonal est in agro Solonio via Ostiensi ad xii lapidem, diverticulo a milliario viii.' The Ager Solonius is brought to the Via Ostiensis and thus to the Tiber, seeing that the road lay along the left bank of the river. The site of Pomonal was located by Lanciani with a fair amount of certainty at Castel Porziano, a mediaeval castle in the Laurentian forest.[3] The eighth milestone, measured from the Servian gate, is to be found at the thirteenth kilometre, near the farmhouse of Malafede, since the old Via Ostiensis was shorter before the river eroded the left bank at Vicus Alexandri and San Ciriaco. Lanciani saw traces of the by-road which he says were studied by other scholars before him, and followed their course to Castel Porziano; he states that the track could

---

[1] Servius, *Ad Aen.*, XI, 317. [2] Festus, *sub voce* '*Pomonal*'.
[3] Lanciani, *M.A.*, 1903, p. 174 sq.

easily be discovered by means of cuttings, remains of paving stones, and ruins of villas along the sides. It crosses the high ground of L'Infermeria, Spagnoletta, and Trefusa. The end of the eight miles indicated by Festus falls where is the mediaeval building, which led Lanciani to conclude that the origin of Castel Porziano was to be recognized not in a Roman *fundus Porcilianus*, but in the very beginnings of Rome, and in the early history of Latium. Pomonal is the only town or city known to have been situated in the Ager Solonius.[1]

Tradition connected with the *ager* goes back to very early times. Macrobius[2] quotes a passage from Cato which gives evidence of this, for in it the mythical Larentia is said to have bequeathed to the Romans certain lands, amongst them the Solonius. Although they represented her profit in her illicit profession, yet the Romans buried her in a splendid tomb, and honoured her with a yearly festival: 'Cato ait Larentiam meretricio questu locupletatam post excessum suum populo Romano agros Turacem, Semurium, Linturium, et Solonium reliquisse, et ideo sepulcri magnificentia et annuae parentationis honore dignatam.' The festival was called the Larentalia and was observed on the twenty-third of December when the high priests, the *pontifices*, offered sacrifices on the altar beside her tomb in the Velabrum. These took the form of funeral rites, as is seen in the use of the word *parentatio* in the passage quoted above, and also in a corresponding notice in the *Fasti Praenestini*.[3] We learn from Varro that the reputed tomb of Larentia was situated at the beginning of the Nova Via,[4] and from Cicero that it was near the Porta Romanula.[5] The feast of Acca Larentia, however, seems a far cry from the Ager Solonius. Her connection with it, traditional or even merely suppositional as it evidently appears, may reflect some early Roman conquest of this part of Latium, or some concession made to the Romans in such early times as to have been forgotten. Lanciani suggests that it was taken from the Etruscans, together with the other *agri* mentioned by Macrobius, and cultivated thereafter by the Laurentians.[6]

As regards the extent of the *ager*, in addition to the data

---

[1] Dion. Hal., *A.R.*, II, 37, speaks of a city called Solonium, Σολωνίου πόλεως, but nothing else is known of it, and the name may be suspect.

[2] Macr., *Sat.*, I, 10, 11.   [3] *C.I.L.*, I, p. 409.   [4] Varro, *L.L.*, VI, 24.

[5] Cic., *Ep. ad Brut.*, I, 15.   [6] *M.A.*, 1903, p. 174 sq.

I*

given by Festus, Plutarch[1] tells how Marius owned a villa there, and that when he was expelled from Rome in 88 B.C. he took refuge in it, and fled thence to Ostia, and made his escape by sea. Here again is implied its western proximity to the Tiber and Ostia. On the other hand, we have evidence for its southern borders, for in telling of a prodigy which happened to the infant Roscius 'in agro Solonio', Cicero adds the explanation: 'qui est campus agri Lanuvini'.[2] These latter words have been suspected by some authorities as an interpolation, but they are to be recognized as sound since they can be corroborated by other literary references. Livy,[3] for instance, records raids made by the Volsci of Antium into the 'Agri Ostiensis, Ardeatis, and Solonius', which suggests that the latter was adjacent to the other two. Cicero makes reference to a villa which he possessed there,[4] and to which he thought of going on occasion to avoid contention in Rome; it is certainly not without significance that in this letter he should couple the Ager Solonius closely with Antium: 'quiescendum, quod non est dissimile atque ire in Solonium, aut Antium'. He also tells us that it abounded in snakes.[5]

As appears then, from the Roman writers themselves, the Ager Solonius was a tract of land bordering on Ostia, Ardea, and Lanuvium, extending, that is, from the Tiber to the southern confines of Latium. This will be found to be compatible with Vergil's description of it. The ancient land, a portion of Latinus' kingdom, is adjacent to the Tiber, for it stretches westward towards the direction in which the sun is seen to set, and touches on the borders of the Sicani: 'fines super usque Sicanos'. These latter words may be understood to refer to the borders of what was later to be Roman territory, or, as we have already seen, to Ficana itself. The first possibility would be in accord with Servius[6] who gives the current belief of his day that Rome was once inhabited by a people calling themselves Sicani, who in their coming ousted the Siculi, the former inhabitants; this is plainly only local tradition, but the interpretation may well be sound: 'usque ad fines [Sicanos] quos Siculi aliquando tenuerunt, id est usque ad ea loca in

---

[1] Plut., *Mar.*, 35.   [2] Cic., *De Div.*, I, 36.
[3] Livy, VIII, 12: *Antiates in agros Ostiensem, Ardeatem, Solonium, incursiones fecerunt.*
[4] Cic., *Ad Att.*, II, 3.   [5] Cic., *De Div.*, ii, 31.
[6] *Ad Aen.*, XI, 317.

quibus nunc Roma est'; if then this be accepted, we may understand that the land stretches to the very borders of future
Rome, and see in these lines a hint of the city that was to be, a
veiled reference, in terms of their supposed forerunners, which
could not fail to please the poet's hearers and the *litterati* of his
circle, and to the situation of Rome which would look back in
posterity to Aeneas as its proto-founder.

The second possible interpretation is the identification with
Ficana. Festus' account of its situation is significant, for he
states that it lay on the eleventh milestone on the Via Ostiensis;
and, according to him also, Pomonal, in the Ager Solonius, lay
at the twelfth. Thus the *ager* may well have bordered on the
territory of ancient Ficana, and these two records can be cited
in strong support of Carcopino's theory. Vergil is, then, preserving a memory of the primitive pre-Ostian port on the last
high ground by the river in a seaward direction, and we may
see in this yet another example of his love of small and humble
places of great antiquity.

The land which is to be Latinus' gift is tilled by two tribes,
the Aurunci and the Rutuli, as his vassals.[1] The Rutuli are the
men of Ardea, therefore the *ager* extends in the direction of
their city, but what can be said of the Aurunci? They were the
people whom the Greeks called Ausones,[2] and were reputed to
be the oldest race in Italy.[3] In early times they had as their city
Aurunca, situated in the mountains on the left of the river
Liris, on a site identified on Monte di Santa Croce, or Rocca
Monfina; later, however, they made their capital at Suessa
Pometia on the south-western slope commanding the plains
stretching westwards to the sea. It is interesting to see that,
in the 'Gathering of the Clans', Vergil[4] describes them as coming from the mountains, giving thus a hint of their earlier
settlement. In history, however, they appear as powerful and
warlike, and as having reached the borders of Latium. In 503
B.C.[5] Cora and Pometia joined them in a revolt, a fact which
would indicate some degree of power and prestige. Later they
allied with their neighbours, the Volsci, and advanced as far as
Aricia. Here they fought a stiff battle against the consul

---

[1] Servius, *Ad Aen.*, XI, 318: *tamquam stipendarium habebant Rutuli et Aurunci, aut
ad quem colendum quasi regi operas dabant.*
[2] *Ibid.*, VII, 727.   [3] *Ibid.*, VII, 206.   [4] *Aen.*, VII, 726-7.
[5] Livy, II, 16, 17.

Servilius, but the Romans were victorious.[1] After this, their
prestige was ended. In 337 B.C.[2] they were so hard pressed by
the Sidicini that they were compelled to ask Rome for help.
It was then that they were driven from their mountain home,
and built their new city of Suessa at the foot of the hills commanding the plains. After this they disappear from history
until 313,[3] when Suessa became a Roman colony.[4]

When, therefore, Latinus names the Aurunci as among the
tillers of his soil, the implication clearly is that 'the antiquus
ager' borders on their territory, that is, on north-western Campania, and on the frontiers of the Volsci and the Aurunci. He
is, then, describing a tract of country stretching across the
middle of the plain of Latium from the Tiber, passing east of
Laurentum and Ardea, and west of Lanuvium, to its southern
extremity on the borders of Campania. With this can be compared, and thus identified, the Ager Solonius, which, as
ancient writers indicate, occupied this part of Latium.

As Latinus describes it, part of the land can be tilled and
part is fit for pasturage; so are the words 'horum asperrima
pascunt' to be understood. He might, indeed, be thought to
suggest that this land is poor, and difficult to work; in fact,
Servius makes the suggestion that he belittles his gift,[5] but this
is incompatible with the occasion, the last desperate effort to
avoid the coming conflict. Latinus is trying to satisfy his own
people, and also to meet the desires of a powerful invader, the
destined husband of his own daughter, as he well knows from
the oracle of Faunus. His gift of so wide a stretch of country
is magnificent enough to satisfy any foreign invader.

Far from disparaging the goodness of the land, he implies
that it is profitable and desirable. Where the top soil of the
Campagna is thin, the soft volcanic rock-strata can be broken
into with the ploughshare; when exposed to weathering agen-
cies the rock disintegrates and forms good soil. Where the
land is not productive, or unfit for tillage, the flocks can be
pastured even as they are to this day. Herein is to be recognized a countryman's whole livelihood, his crops and his flocks.
Where the land will not bear, it will at least afford grazing

---

[1] Livy, II, 26; Dion. Hal., *A.R.*, VI, 32.   [2] Livy, VII, 28; VIII, 15.
[3] Livy, IX, 28.
[4] This account is taken from the *Dictionary of Greek and Roman Geography*, 1857;
see also Pauly-Wissowa, *Real-Encyclopadie*, III², p. 981.
[5] Servius, *Ad Aen.*, XI, 319: *extenuat agri meritum.*

ground. The stress in Latinus' words is on 'colles', not on 'duros', and on 'pascunt', not on 'asperrima'.

The Campagna country is partly cultivated and partly pasture, as Vergil describes it. In the Ager Solonius are found the lower outcrops of the volcanic rock of the Alban Hills, the ridge known as the Monte di Decima. Seen from the plains, on the Laurentian shore, they appear to be much higher than they really are; the ridge wooded with pines is true to the locality, for many screens of woodland are to be seen on the Campagna, especially along this higher ground.

Thus understood, this passage is found to be a faithful description of the country inland from Ardea and Laurentum, showing how well the poet knew the aspect of the scene. Furthermore, it may be asked what was his peculiar interest in this ancient territory, but the answer remains obscure. Two famous Romans had villas there, Marius and Cicero, and others unknown to us may have done so too. There was a tradition which connected it with an ancient cult in Rome, and with Rome's early history, but more than this our present knowledge will not allow us to conjecture. The passage, then, is to be understood thus: 'I have an ancient land, the one nearest the Tuscan stream, stretching far to the sunset, even to the confines of the Sicani; the Aurunci and the Rutuli till it, and work the hard slopes with the ploughshare, and pasture their flocks on those parts barren to the plough. Let all this region, and the pine-wooded tract of the high ridge be given to the Trojans in friendship.'

BIBLIOGRAPHY

ÅBERG, N.	*Bronzezeitliche und Früheisenzeitliche Chronologie*, I, Italien, 1930.
ALTHEIM, F.	*Grieschiche Götter im alten Rom*, 1930.
ASHBY, T.	*Classical Topography of the Roman Campagna*, *B.S.R.*, 1902, 1910. *J.R.S.*, 1912. *The Roman Campagna in Classical Times*, 1927.
BAILEY, C.	*Religion in Vergil*, 1935.
BENDZ	*Opuscula Archaeologica*, I, 1934[1].
BOAS, H.	*Aeneas' Arrival in Latium, Allard Pierson Stichting Archaeologisch-Historische Bydragen*, VI, 1938.
BOËTHIUS, A.	*B.M.*, 1931, 1934. *Roma*, IX, 1931.
BONSTETTEN, C. V. DE	*Voyage dans le Latium* (1st edition, 1805; 2nd edition, 1861).
CALZA, G.	*Guida di Ostia*, 1924. *N.S.*, 1914, 1923.
CARCOPINO, J.	*Virgile et les Origines d'Ostie*, 1919.
CLUVERIUS	*Italia Antiqua*, 1624.
CORPUS INSCRIPTIONUM LATINARUM, 1887.	
FOWLER, W. WARDE	*J.R.S.*, 1911. *Roman Festivals of the Republic*, 1899. *Religious Experience of the Roman People*, 1911.
FRANK, TENNY	*American Journal of Philology*, XLV, 1924. *Economic History of Rome*, 1927.
GELL, W.	*Topography of Rome and its Vicinity*, 1842 (2nd edition).
HARE, A. J. C.	*Walks Round Rome*, 1906.
JEX-BLAKE, K., & SELLERS, E.	*The Elder Pliny's Chapters on the History of Art*, 1896.
KNIGHT, W. F. J.	*Cumaean Gates*, 1936. *Roman Vergil*, 1944.
LANCIANI, R.	*M.A.*, 1903. *Wanderings in the Roman Campagna*, 1909.

Last, H.	*C.A.H.*, vol. VII, 1928.
Lugli, G.	*Historia*, VII.
Malten, L.	*Aineias, Archiv für Religionswissenschaft,* 1931-2.
McIver, R.	*Villanovans and Early Etruscans,* 1924. *Iron Age in Italy,* 1927.
Nibby, A.	*Analisi della Carta dei Dintorni di Roma,* 1848 (2nd edition).
Paribeni, R.	*M.A.,* 1911.
Pasqui, A.	*N.S.,* 1900.
Perrone	*Carta idrografica d'Italia,* 1908.
Piganiol, .A	*La Conquête Romaine,* 1927.
Platner, S. B. & Ashby, T.	*Topographical Dictionary of Rome,* 1929.
Rehm, B.	*Das geographische Bild des alten Italiens in Virgils Aeneis,* 1932 (Philologus Supplementband, XXIV, Heft II).
Richter, O.	*Annali dell' Istituto,* 1884.
Säflund, G.	*Le Mura di Roma Repubblicana,* 1932.
Saunders, C.	*Vergil's Primitive Italy,* 1930.
Tomassetti, G. & F.	*La Campagna Romana,* 1910.
Vaglieri, D.	*Boll. Com.,* 1911.
Van Buren, E. D.	*Figurative Terracotta Revetments in Etruria and Latium,* 1921.
Villari, L.	*On the Roads from Rome,* 1932.
Volpi	*Vetus Latium Profanum,* 1734.
Von Duhn	*Italische Gräberkunde,* Erster Teil, 1924.

ABBREVIATIONS USED IN THE TEXT

A.I.	*Annali dell' Istituto.*
A.J.P.	*American Journal of Philology.*
B.M.	*Bollettino dell' Associazione Internazionale degli Studi Mediterranei.*
Boll. Com.	*Bollettino della Commissione Archeologica.*
B.P.I.	*Bollettino Paletnologico Italiano.*
B.S.R.	*Papers of the British School at Rome.*
C.A.H.	*Cambridge Ancient History.*
C.I.L.	*Corpus Inscriptionum Latinarum.*
Dion. Hal., *A.R.*	Dionysius of Halicarnassus, *Antiquitates Romanae.*
J.R.S.	*Journal of Roman Studies.*
M.A.	*Monumenti Antichi.*
N.H.	*Naturalis Historia.*
N.S.	*Notizie degli Scavi.*
V.O.O.	Carcopino, *Virgile et les Origines d'Ostie,* 1919.